Copyright © 2012 Bernard J. Lawson Jr.

All rights reserved.

ISBN-13: 978-1456369651
ISBN-10: 1456369652

PREFACE

Do you know what's required to get your Texas CHL?

Do you remember what you were taught during the CHL class?

Do you understand each provision of the Texas Concealed handgun Licensing Act (Texas Government Code Chapter 411, Subchapter H) that creates an offense under the laws of the State of Texas and each provision of the laws of the State of Texas related to use of deadly force?

The purpose of this guide is to help those who currently hold a Texas Concealed Handgun License (CHL) or who are seeking to obtain a Texas CHL understand what's required to get, sustain, and renew the CHL. This guide can also assist Texas Department of Public Safety (DPS) Qualified instructors for CHL training.

This guide lists some of the Texas Concealed Handgun Laws and selected Statutes that all Texas and Non-Texas Resident CHL holders must know while carrying in the State of Texas.

Also included are the laws created and amended as a result of the passage of bills by the 2011 Regular Session of the 82nd Texas Legislature. The changes in the laws contained in this pamphlet became effective September 1, 2011, unless otherwise noted.

The contents of this guide are not affiliated or endorsed by TX DPS as DPS does not endorse any commercial enterprise. This guide is a collection of information gathered and presented by a TX DPS Certified CHL Instructor. All inquiries should be directed to: Bernard@TexasCHLacademy.com.

.

CONTENTS

Acknowledgments

The Texas Concealed Handgun License (CHL)	Pg 8
How to apply for the Texas CHL	Pg 12
CHL Photograph Requirements	Pg 17
CHL fees/ Special Conditions and required documentation	Pg 19
Non-Resident Texas CHL	Pg 48
Eligibility Requirements	Pg 50
The CHL Application Process	Pg 71
The CHL Course/Shooting Requirements	Pg 74
Confidentiality of Records	Pg 86
Change of Address or Name	Pg 88
Modification of the CHL	Pg 90
Length of CHL License	Pg 91
The CHL Renewal Process	Pg 92

Rights of Employers	Pg 96
Displaying a CHL on a peace officer demand	Pg 102
What to do during traffic stops	Pg 103
Authority of peace officer to disarm	Pg 104
Places where concealed carry is not authorized	Pg 107
Unlawful carrying by a CHL holder	Pg 110
Trespass by a CHL holder	Pg 115
Making a firearm accessible to a child	Pg 118
CHL agreements with other states	Pg 121
Suspension or Revocation of CHL	Pg 128
CHL Denial, Revocation or Suspension Review Process	Pg 131
Use Of Force	Pg 134
Selected Deadly Force Statues	Pg 137
Confinement as Justifiable	Pg 138
Threats as Justifiable Force	Pg 138
Reckless Injury of Innocent Third Person	Pg 138
Civil Remedies Unaffected	Pg 139
Public Duty	Pg 140

Necessity	Pg 141
Self Defense	Pg 141
Deadly Force in Defense of a Person	Pg 145
Defense of a Third Person	Pg 147
Protection of Life or Health	Pg 147
Protection of one's own Property	Pg 148
Deadly Force to Protect Property	Pg 149
Protection of a Third Person's Property	Pg 151
Use of Device to Protect Property	Pg 152
Non-Violent Communication	Pg 153
How to contact the Texas DPS	Pg 167
Laws Relating to the Texas CHL Quick Reference	Pg 168

Texas Concealed Handgun Guide 2012

ACKNOWLEDGMENTS

First I would like to thank Mr. James Daywalt for his encouragement to develop this guide.

Words alone cannot express the thanks I owe to Jovanka, my girlfriend, for her encouragement, patience and assistance for allowing me to take the time to accomplish this guide.

Special thanks to Mr. Ben Lively and Mr. Bobby McMillan at Blackhawk Shooting Range for their expert instruction on firearms and for providing me with the resources to provide such an outstanding CHL course at San Antonio's most progressive shooting range.

Thanks to Mr. Brady Calloway for assisting with the CHL Course and Mr. P.J. Hermosa for providing outstanding briefings about the Texas Law Shield Program™ during each course.

The Texas Concealed Handgun License (CHL)

The Texas Concealed Handgun License began when the Seventy-Fourth Legislative session passed Senate Bill 60, "The Right-to-Carry law" and was signed by former Governor of Texas George W. Bush on May 26, 1995. The law became effective for the State of Texas on September 1, 1995. As of January 1, 1996, Texas residents can exercise a license to carry a concealed handgun as long as they meet the eligibility requirements, pass the background investigation and complete all required paperwork and pass the concealed handgun proficiency course requirements.

The State of Texas allows most individuals the right to carry a concealed handgun as long as they apply for, meet the fourteen eligibility requirements, pass the background investigation and pass a CHL certification course and receive a Form CHL- 100 certificate signed by the applicant and a qualified CHL instructor.

The issuance of a CHL is a benefit to the license holder for the purposes of those sections of the Penal Code to which the definition of "Benefit" under Section 1.07, Penal Code, applies.

"Benefit" means anything reasonably regarded as economic gain or advantage including benefit to any other person in whose welfare the beneficiary is interested. Therefore the State of Texas will issue a CHL to those who qualify.

People have always had the right to keep and bear arms under the Second Amendment to the United States Constitution. The intentions of the Constitution were very clear at the time it was drafted and the founders of the United States were very clear in their intent. Thomas Jefferson, James Madison, Samuel Adams, Alexander Hamilton and Patrick Henry all have provided great quotes as to their intent.

The right to keep and bear arms was passed down to all the states in the union. Most states have the right to keep and bear arms imbedded in their own Constitutions, often written more clearly than the U.S. Bill of Rights.

Below is an excerpt from the Constitution of the State of Texas, Article 1, Section 23: Right to Keep and Bear Arms:

"Every citizen shall have the right to keep and bear arms in the lawful defense of himself or the State; but the Legislature shall have power, by law, to regulate the wearing of arms, with a view to prevent crime."

Today the topic of discussion on guns is very controversial. There are many special interest groups on both sides of the fence on the topic of guns. This guide will not cover the controversial issues. This guide will focus on the State of Texas and will cover Subchapter H, Chapter 411 of the Government Code (The Concealed Handgun Law) and related Statues.

First, let's start with some of the basics about firearms and the State of Texas. To purchase a gun you will need a valid state-issued ID. There is no requirement to register a firearm in the state. So if you purchased, inherited, or have been given a firearm there is no need to transfer it into your name. A person also cannot openly carry a handgun unless you are on your own property, hunting or in the commission of a sporting event (i.e. shooting range, shooting competition etc). There is no open carry law in the State of Texas.

To carry a handgun on your person, you must have a CHL. You may however, carry a loaded handgun in your vehicle without having a CHL under the newly passed Motorist Protection Act. More information about carrying in a motor vehicle is covered under the Texas Penal Code 46.02 in this guide. There is also no limit on how many bullets a person is allowed to load into magazines in the State of Texas which means you can load as many as you wish.

As far as long guns (i.e. shotguns and rifles) are concerned, you are allowed to possess in a motor vehicle and they don't have to be concealed.

The CHL process involves two basic steps. Although each step has intricacies involved, here are the two basic steps:

> A. Complete the online CHL application process through the DPS website, and
>
> B. Complete a Texas CHL course taught by a qualified CHL instructor with a current license to teach and obtain a Form CHL-100 certificate from the instructor at the end of the course.

The process is relatively straight forward. Now let's look at how to apply in a little more detail.

How to apply

An applicant seeking a Texas CHL has three options available when it comes to applying.

Option 1- Apply Online

This is the preferred method. DPS has a great user friendly website where you can apply for a new or renewal CHL application electronically. Applicants can take full control of the application process, from beginning to end just by visiting the Texas Department of Public Safety's Website: **www.txdps.state.tx.us**, click on the online services tab, and then click on the Concealed Handgun Licensing Bureau.

From the website applicants can:

- Submit the application fee
- Complete and submit the CHL web based application
- Schedule electronic fingerprints
- Find a CHL Instructor and take the CHL course

When you are ready to complete the online application you will need to have the following information readily available:

- Valid credit card (Visa, MasterCard, Discover, or American Express).

- Social security number,
- Valid driver license or identification card,
- Current demographic, address, contact, and employment information,
- Residential and employment information for the last five years (new users only),
- Information regarding any psychiatric, drug, alcohol, or criminal history (new users only) and,
- A valid email address.

Scheduling for fingerprint submission will take place during the online application process. Just follow the simple and easy to read instructions on the screen. The Texas Administrative Rules relating to CHL was amended and became effective on January 9, 2011 stated that effective March 1, 2011, DPS require applicants to submit electronic fingerprints with original applications. DPS will attempt to utilize existing prints on file for renewal applications however, if the prints on file do not meet current quality standards, new fingerprints must be submitted electronically through the L-1 Enrollment Service (L-1). (Note: read option 2 for fingerprinting fees and payment options).

L-1 currently has fingerprint locations available across the state of Texas. During scheduling through the DPS website, the applicant will select the location, date and time that is most convenient for them to get fingerprinted. When fingerprinted using L-1, your prints are electronically transferred to DPS and the FBI. Electronic fingerprints are preferred due to their 98% classifiability rate which results in fewer fingerprint quality rejections.

When you complete the application process through the DPS website electronically you will print off a page entitled "checklist of documents" which lists what required documents you will need to return back to DPS in order to process your request for the CHL.

Option 2- Download the CHL Application & Forms yourself. Applicants who aren't sure about applying online can still take advantage of DPS's online resources. Those who wish to submit a paper copy application can download the required forms needed under downloadable forms on the left hand side of the DPS CHL main webpage.

- Download, print and fill out the paper application and supplemental forms
- Find a CHL Instructor and take the CHL course

Because each individual may apply under different circumstances, specific requirements are listed under each special condition. Below is a short list of the required documents that are part of the Texas CHL packet:

- Form CHL-78A CHL Application
- Form CHL-78B Address & Business History
- Form CHL-78C Reported History
- Form CHL-85 Release of Records Affidavit
- Form CHL-86 Knowledge of Laws & Eligibility Affidavit
- Form CHL-6 Photo Holder/ID Signature form
- Two color passport type photos

- CHL-100 Handgun Proficiency Certificate (provided by a CHL Instructor)

You cannot be fingerprinted until the L-1 can verify you in the TX DPS computer database. It would be wise to call DPS to ensure that your application information is entered in the computer system before getting fingerprinted through L-1.

CHL applicants <u>must have done one of the following</u> to schedule an appointment for fingerprinting with L-1:

1. An <u>online application</u> must have been submitted, Or
2. TXDPS must be in receipt of the paper CHL application.

The fingerprint processing fee is currently set at $9.95, payable to L-1 online with a credit card **or** at the L-1 location where the payment <u>must</u> be made by check or money order only.

Complete the application process by mailing in the paper application, supplemental documents, any applicable fees, fingerprints, color photos and the CHL-100 form obtained from a DPS qualified CHL instructor.

Keep in mind that the paper submitted copies require additional time to process. If your handwriting is not legible, it may cause your application to be delayed. It's a good idea to print legibly so that your paperwork can be entered into the computer database properly.

Option 3- is One Stop Shopping with a CHL Instructor. However, fingerprinting still must be accomplished through the Fingerprint Application Service of Texas (FAST) unless the instructor is an authorized agent using the FAST. It is also important to remember that the fees charged by CHL instructors to attend the required certification course and fees charged by L-1 are totally separate from the application license fees paid directly to DPS.

CHL Photographs Requirements

Photographs are required with original concealed handgun license applications. Photographs are not required for renewal applications or instructor-only applications as long as the existing photograph on file with the department meets quality standards. Applicants may be required to submit new or an updated photograph if the existing photographs do not meet quality standards or the applicant's appearance has changed such that identification is inhibited.

If an applicant is required to submit new or updated photographs, the applicant shall submit two identical photographs of the applicant to the department. The photographs must be un-retouched color prints.

Snapshots, vending machine prints, and full length photographs will not be accepted. The photographs must be 2 inches by 2 inches in size and printed on photo quality paper. The photographs must be taken in normal light, with a contrasting white, off-white, or blue background. The photographs must present a good likeness of the applicant taken within the last six months. Unless worn daily for religious purposes, all hats or headgear must be removed for the photograph and no item or attire may cover or otherwise obscure any facial features (eyes, nose, and mouth).

Eyeglasses must be removed for the photograph. The photographs must present a clear, frontal image of the applicant and include the full face from the bottom of the chin to the top of the head, including hair. The image of the applicant must be between 1 and 1-3/8 inches.

Only the applicant may be portrayed. Photographs in which the faces of the person being photographed are not in focus will not be accepted. Upon development of an interface allowing the Regulatory Services Division to access the photographs on file with the Driver License Division system or development of other electronic means to obtain the applicant's photograph, applicants may not be required to submit printed photographs.

Most CHL Instructors will provide you with photos. Check with your instructor to see if they provide photo services.

Texas CHL Fees/Special Conditions and required documentation

The standard application license fee to apply for the Texas CHL is currently set at $140 and is paid directly to the Texas Department of Public Safety at the time you submit your application.

If you complete your application online you will be prompted to enter your credit card number. The Texas DPS application fee is non-refundable, so please read the eligibility requirements carefully before applying.

You may qualify for a discounted rate under the special conditions category.

It's important to remember that if you submit your application under one of the special conditions, you will be required to provide proof of eligibility under that specific special condition.

Special Conditions

TXDPS provides a discounted application license fee if a person applying for the CHL qualify under one of the special conditions. Listed below are the special condition categories. DPS fees are subject to change so check the DPS website for the most current information in regards to fees. The applicant fees listed are current as of the publication date of this guide.

- Active Military $0.00 or Discharged within the last year, the fee is waived. $0.00

- Military Veteran $70.00 for a new applicant and $35.00 for renewal

- Senior Citizen $70.00 for a new applicant and $35.00 for renewal

- Indigent Person $70.00 for a new applicant and $35.00 for renewal

- Active Texas Peace Officer $25.00 for a new applicant and $25.00 for renewal

- Honorably Retired Texas Peace Officer $25.00 for a new applicant and $25.00 for renewal

- Retired Federal Agent $25.00for a new applicant and $25.00 for renewal

- Active Judicial Officer $25.00 for a new applicant and $25.00 for renewal

- Retired Judicial Officer $25.00 for a new applicant and $25.00 for renewal

- Elected Felony Prosecuting Attorney the fee is waived $0.00/$0.00

- Assistant Prosecuting Attorney/Other $140.00 for a new applicant and $70.00 for renewal

If you qualify for one of the special conditions, you will need to include the necessary documentation to support your claim. Let's take a closer look at what's required for each special condition.

Active Military

Military personnel now stationed in Texas, just like civilians, may obtain a concealed handgun license as soon as they arrive. It is no longer required that the individual reside in Texas for six months prior to applying.

TX DPS waives the fee for the issuance of an original, duplicate, modified, or renewed CHL license if the applicant for the license is a member of the United States Armed Forces, including a member of the Reserves, National Guard, or State Guard. Therefore there is no charge for the application license fee however; the fee to take the CHL course still applies. The minimum age for active military to request a Texas CHL is 18 years of age however, the issuance of a license to carry a concealed handgun to a person eligible under Subsection (g) does not affect the person's ability to purchase a handgun or ammunition under federal law. Persons under 21 years of age may not purchase a handgun or ammunition from a Federal Firearms Dealer. See 18 U.S.C. §922(x) (1).

It is recommended that the application is completed online. However, if a person wishes to submit a hard copy paper application be sure to download all required documents from the DPS website.

In accordance with Texas Government Code §411.1881, a person may not be required to complete the range instruction portion of the handgun proficiency course to obtain or renew a CHL issued if the person:

- Is currently serving in or is honorably discharged from:
    - The Army, Navy, Air Force, Coast Guard, or Marines Corps of the United States or an auxiliary service or reserve unit of one of those branches of the armed forces; or
    - The state military forces, as defined by Section 431.001; **and**

Has, within the five years preceding the date of the person's application for an original or renewed license, as applicable, completed a course of training in handgun proficiency or familiarization as part of the person's service with the armed forces or state military forces".

The exemption only allows an exemption from the range portion of the concealed handgun course. Exempted military personnel must still take the classroom portion and the written examination.

If you complete your application online through the DPS website you will be prompted to print off a checklist of documents form. This particular form has a barcode on it and will let the applicant know what documents to return to DPS for processing.

If you wish to submit a paper copy application here is a list of the required documentation you will need to submit to DPS:

- Fee waived-$0
- Form CHL-78A CHL Application
- Form CHL-78B Address & Business History
- Form CHL-78C Reported History
- Form CHL-85 Release of Records Affidavit
- Form CHL-86 Knowledge of Laws & Eligibility Affidavit
- Form CHL-6 Photo Holder/ID Signature form
- Two color passport type photos
- Electronic Fingerprints through L-1
- Military range scores from within the last five years (if substituting range scores in place of proficiency portion of training with CHL Instructor
- A copy of Military ID card
- A current copy of Leave Earnings Statement or current orders or letter from Commanding Officer verifying Military status
- Born out of country supplemental documentation that meets the requirements listed on the notice from CHL-40 (if born out of the United States)
- A clear, front and back, color copy of your state issued ID/DL (if issued by a state other than Texas)

- CHL-100 Proficiency Certificate- provided by a CHL instructor.

Ref: Texas GC §411.1881, GC§411.1951, GC§411.185 (a) (1) and GC§411.185 (a) (2)).

Military Veteran

Texas DPS waives or reduces the fees for veterans of United States Armed Forces. New Applicant fee: $70. Renewal fee: $35.

A "veteran" means a person who:

- Has served in the army, navy, air force, coast guard, or marine corps of the United States;
- The state military forces as defined by Section 431.001;or
- An auxiliary service of one of those branches of the armed forces; and
- Has been honorably discharged from the branch of the service in which the person served.

DPS will waive the fee if the veteran, within 365 days preceding the date of the application, was honorably discharged from the branch of service in which the person served.

If it has been more than 365 days since the veteran was honorably discharged, DPS reduces the fee by 50 percent for the issuance of an original, duplicate, modified, or renewed license.

If you complete your application online through the DPS website you will be prompted to print off a checklist of documents form. This form has a barcode on it and will let you know what documents to return to DPS for processing.

If you submit a paper copy application with the military veteran special condition, here is a list of the required documentation you will need to submit to DPS:

- Form CHL-78A CHL Application
- Form CHL-78B Address & Business History
- Form CHL-78C Reported History
- Form CHL-85 Release of Records Affidavit
- Form CHL-86 Knowledge of Laws & Eligibility Affidavit
- Form CHL-6 Photo Holder/ID Signature form
- Two color passport type photos
- Electronic Fingerprints through L-1
- A copy of DD-214 Member 4 copy, or other official document showing honorable discharge from the military and retired military credentials
- Applicable Fee (in the form of a personal check, cashier's check, money order
- Born out of country supplemental documentation that meets the requirements listed on the notice form CHL-40 (if born out of the United States)
- A clear, front and back, color copy of your state issued ID/DL (if issued by a state other than Texas)
- Form CHL-100 Proficiency Certificate.

You may be eligible to use your military range scores from within the last five years if substituting range scores in place of proficiency portion of training with CHL Instructor.

Ref: Texas GC §411.1881, GC§411.1951, GC§411.185 (a) (1) and GC§411.185 (a) (2)).

Senior Citizen

DPS reduces the fees for senior citizens by 50 percent for the issuance of an original, duplicate, modified, or renewed license.

Applicants claiming Senior Citizen status must be of 60 years of age or older at the time of application as shown on their Texas Drivers License or State ID card.

If you complete your application online through the DPS website you will be prompted to print off a checklist of documents form. This form has a barcode on it and will let you know what documents to return to DPS for processing.

If you submit a paper copy application here is a list of the required documentation you will need to submit to DPS:

- New Applicant Fee -$70 Renewal Fee $35
- Form CHL-78A CHL Application
- Form CHL-78B Address & Business History
- Form CHL-78C Reported History
- Form CHL-85 Release of Records Affidavit
- Form CHL-86 Knowledge of Laws & Eligibility Affidavit
- Form CHL-6 Photo Holder/ID Signature form
- Two color passport type photos

- Electronic Fingerprints through L-1
- Form CHL 100-Profiency Certificate- Provided by CHL Instructor after completion of course.

    Ref: Texas GC§411.195.

Indigent Person

DPS reduces the fee by 50 percent for the issuance of an original, duplicate, modified, or renewed license if the department determines that the applicant is indigent.

An applicant requesting a reduction of fees is required to submit proof of indigence with the application materials submitted to DPS.

Applicants claiming indigent status must submit a copy of their previous year Internal Revenue Service tax return. Indigence is determined by examining the size of the family unit and the yearly income level of the family unit.

An applicant is determined to be indigent if the applicant's income in not more than 100 percent of the applicable income level established by the following federal poverty guidelines:

2011 HHS Poverty Guidelines

Persons in Family	48 Contiguous States and D.C.	Alaska	Hawaii
1	$10.890	$13,600	$12,540
2	17,710	18,380	16,930
3	18,530	23,160	21,320
4	22,350	27,940	25,710
5	26,170	32,720	30,100
6	29,990	37,500	34,490
7	33,810	42,280	38,880
8	37,630	47,060	43,270
For each additional person, add	3,820	4,780	4,390

SOURCE: *Federal Register*, Vol. 76, No. 13, January 20, 2011, pp. 3637-3638.

If you complete your application online through the DPS website you will be prompted to print off a form titled *"checklist of documents"*. This form has a barcode on it and will let you know what documents that will need to be returned to DPS for processing.

If you submit a paper copy application under the special condition of Indigent, here is a list of the required documentation you will need to submit to DPS:

- New Applicant Fee -$70 Renewal Fee $35
- Form CHL-78A CHL Application

- Form CHL-78B Address & Business History
- Form CHL-78C Reported History
- Form CHL-85 Release of Records Affidavit
- Form CHL-86 Knowledge of Laws & Eligibility Affidavit
- Form CHL-6 Photo Holder/ID Signature form
- Two color passport type photos
- Electronic Fingerprints through L-1
- IRS Tax Return
- Form CHL 100-Profiency Certificate- Provided by CHL Instructor after completion of course.

Ref: Texas GC §411.194.

Active Peace Officer

A person who is licensed as a peace officer under Chapter 1701, Occupations Code, and is employed full-time as a peace officer by a law enforcement agency may apply for a license. (Ref: GC§411.1991). The applicant must submit electronic fingerprints through L-1 Enrollment Services and a sworn statement from the head of the law enforcement agency employing the applicant.

This statement must include: The name and rank of the applicant, whether or not the applicant has been accused of misconduct at any time during the applicant's period of employment and the disposition of that accusation, a description of the physical and mental condition of the applicant, a list of the types of handguns the applicant had demonstrated proficiency with during the preceding year and a recommendation from the agency head that a license be issued to the person under this article. All information under §411.1991(a) Texas Government Code is required.

If the application is completed online through the DPS website the applicant will be prompted to print off a checklist of documents form. This form has a barcode on it and will let you know what documents to return to DPS for processing.

If you submit a paper copy application here is a list of the required documentation you will need to submit to DPS:

- New Applicant Fee -$25 Renewal Fee $25
- Form CHL-78A CHL Application
- Form CHL-85 Release of Records Affidavit
- Form CHL-86 Knowledge of Laws & Eligibility Affidavit
- Form CHL-6 Photo Holder/ID Signature form
- Two color passport type photos
- Electronic Fingerprints through L-1
- Statement meeting requirements of GC§411.1991(a)
- Born out of country supplemental documentation that meets the requirements listed on the notice form CHL-40 (if born out of the United States)
- A clear, front and back, color copy of your state issued ID/DL (if issued by a state other than Texas)

Active commissioned peace officers are exempt from taking the handgun proficiency course.

Honorably Retired Texas Peace Officer

To be eligible under this category an applicant must have been licensed as a peace officer under Chapter 415, Texas Government Code and must have been employed as a full-time peace officer by a law enforcement agency. To be considered "honorably retired" an applicant must not have retired in lieu of any disciplinary action, must have been eligible to retire from the law enforcement agency (or must have been ineligible to retire only as a result of an injury received in the course of employment), and must be entitled to receive a pension or annuity for service as a law enforcement officer (or not entitled to a pension or annuity only because the law enforcement agency does not offer a pension or annuity to its employees).

Applicants for this category can apply at any time after retirement. The applicant must submit electronic fingerprints and a sworn statement from the head of the law enforcement agency employing the applicant.

This statement must include: The name and rank of the applicant, the status of the applicant before retirement, the applicant's dates of employment with the agency, whether or not the applicant was accused of misconduct at the time of the retirement, the physical and mental condition of the applicant, the type of handguns the applicant had demonstrated proficiency with during the last year of employment, whether the applicant would be eligible for re-employment with the agency, and if not, the reasons the applicant is not eligible and a recommendation from the agency head regarding the issuance of a license under this article.

A retired peace officer who obtains a license under this subchapter must maintain, for the category of weapon licensed, the proficiency required for a peace officer under Texas GC Section 415.035.

The proficiency shall be reported to the Department upon application and renewal.

(Government Code section 415.035 was re-codified during the 1999 legislative session and may now be found in Occupations Code Section 1701.355.)

- New Applicant Fee -$25 Renewal Fee $25
- Form CHL-78A CHL Application
- Form CHL-85 Release of Records Affidavit
- Form CHL-86 Knowledge of Laws & Eligibility Affidavit
- Form CHL-6 Photo Holder/ID Signature form
- Two color passport type photos
- Electronic Fingerprints through L-1
- Statement meeting requirements of Texas GC§411.1991(a)

- Born out of country supplemental documentation that meets the requirements listed on the notice form CHL-40 (if born out of the United States)
- A clear, front and back, color copy of your state issued ID/DL (if issued by a state other than Texas)

Retired law enforcement officers are exempt from taking the handgun proficiency course. However, they must demonstrate weapons proficiency annually through a law enforcement agency.

Ref: Texas GC§411.199

Retired Federal Officer

To qualify in this category an applicant must be a retired officer of the United States who was eligible to carry a firearm in the discharge of his official duties. Applicants for this category may apply any time after their retirement.

The applicant must submit with the application retirement credentials and a letter from the agency head stating the applicant retired in good standing.

- New Applicant Fee -$25 Renewal Fee $25
- Form CHL-78A CHL Application
- Form CHL-85 Release of Records Affidavit
- Form CHL-86 Knowledge of Laws & Eligibility Affidavit
- Form CHL-6 Photo Holder/ID Signature form
- Two color passport type photos
- Electronic Fingerprints through L-1
- Retirement Credentials GC§411.199(g)(2)
- Letter of retirement in good standing GC§411.199(g)(2)
- Born out of country supplemental documentation that meets the requirements listed on the notice form CHL-40 (if born out of the United States)

- A clear, front and back, color copy of your state issued ID/DL (if issued by a state other than Texas).

    Ref: Texas GC§411.201

Active Judicial Officer

A person who is serving in the State of Texas as a judge or justice of a federal court, or as an active judicial officer as defined by Section 411.201 may established handgun proficiency by obtaining from a handgun proficiency instructor approved by the Commission on Law Enforcement Officer Standards and Education for purposes of Section 1702.1675, Occupations Code, a sworn statement that:

- Indicates that the person, during the 12-month period preceding the date of the person's application to the department, demonstrated to the instructor proficiency in the use of handguns; and
- Designates the categories of handguns with respect to which the person demonstrated proficiency

A license issued under this section automatically expires on the six-month anniversary of the date the person's status under

Subsection (a) becomes inapplicable. A license that expires under this subsection may be renewed under Section 411.185.

These applicants will be verified manually on a case by case basis using information provided in the application.

If you complete your application online through the DPS website you will be prompted to print off a checklist of documents form. This form has a barcode on it and will let you know what documents to return to DPS for processing.

> If you submit a paper copy application under this special condition here is a list of the required documentation you will need to submit to DPS:

- New Applicant Fee -$25 Renewal Fee $25
- Form CHL-78A CHL Application
- Form CHL-85 Release of Records Affidavit
- Form CHL-86 Knowledge of Laws & Eligibility Affidavit
- Form CHL-6 Photo Holder/ID Signature form
- Two color passport type photos
- Electronic Fingerprints through L-1
- CHL-100 (proficiency only, not required on renewal if you meet GC§411.185 (a)(1) and GC§411.185 (a)(2)) or submit a sworn statement meeting GC§411.1882
- Sworn Statement meeting GC§411.1882 (if not showing proficiency with a CHL instructor with form CHL-100)
- Statement verifying employment preferred

- Born out of country supplemental documentation that meets the requirements listed on the notice form CHL-40 (if born out of the United States)
- A clear, front and back, color copy of your state issued ID/DL (if issued by a state other than Texas).

State and federal judicial officers must take an abbreviated course covering handgun proficiency and safe storage.

Ref: Texas GC§411.201

Retired Judicial Officer

The applicants under this special condition will be verified manually on a case by case basis using information provided in the application. Ref: Texas GC§411.201.

If you complete your application online through the DPS website you will be prompted to print the "checklist of documents" form. The form has a barcode on it and will let you know what documents to return to DPS for processing.

If you submit a paper copy application under this here is the list of the required documents needed to submit to DPS:

- New Applicant Fee -$25 Renewal Fee $25
- Form CHL-78A CHL Application
- Form CHL-85 Release of Records Affidavit
- Form CHL-86 Knowledge of Laws & Eligibility Affidavit
- Form CHL-6 Photo Holder/ID Signature form
- Two color passport type photos
- Electronic Fingerprints through L-1
- CHL-100 (not required on renewal if you meet GC§411.185 (a)(1) and GC§411.185 (a)(2))
- Statement verifying retired status preferred

- Born out of country supplemental documentation that meets the requirements listed on the notice form CHL-40 (if born out of the United States)
- A clear, front and back, color copy of your state issued ID/DL (if issued by a state other than Texas).

Assistant Prosecuting Attorney/Other

If you complete your application online through the DPS website you will be prompted to print off a checklist of documents form. This form has a barcode on it and will let you know what documents to return to DPS for processing. If you submit a paper copy application under this special condition here is a list of the required documentation you will need to submit to DPS:

- New Applicant Fee -$140 Renewal Fee $70
- Form CHL-78A CHL Application
- Form CHL-85 Release of Records Affidavit
- Form CHL-86 Knowledge of Laws & Eligibility Affidavit
- Form CHL-6 Photo Holder/ID Signature form
- Two color passport type photos
- Electronic Fingerprints through L-1
- CHL-100 (proficiency only, not required on renewal if you meet GC§411.185 (a)(1) and GC§411.185 (a)(2)) or submit a sworn statement meeting GC§411.1882
- Sworn Statement meeting GC§411.1882 (if not showing proficiency with a CHL instructor with form CHL-100)
- Statement verifying employment preferred

- Born out of country supplemental documentation that meets the requirements listed on the notice form CHL-40 (if born out of the United States) A clear, front and back, color copy of your state issued ID/DL (if issued by a state other than Texas)

    Ref: Texas GC§411.179(c), GC§411.1882

Non-Resident Texas Concealed Handgun License

As of September 1, 2005 under Texas House Bill 225 a legal resident of another state can apply for the Texas CHL. Non-Residents must meet all eligibility criteria except the residency requirement. Non-Residents must submit a color copy front and back of their State issued identification or driver's license. In addition, Non-Resident applicants must include addresses and phone numbers for the local police department, sheriff's office and county tax assessor in the county of their non-Texas, primary residence.

New CHL Applicant fee $140. Renewal fee $70.
- Form CHL-78A CHL Application
- Form CHL-78B Address & Business History
- Form CHL-78C Reported History
- Form CHL-85 Release of Records Affidavit
- Form CHL-86 Knowledge of Laws & Eligibility Affidavit
- Form CHL-6 Photo Holder/ID Signature form
- Color copy, front and back, of your state issued identification or drivers license.

You will also need to submit two color passport type photos, Form CHL-100 which is the handgun proficiency certificate provided by a qualified CHL instructor after completion of the Texas CHL course and the applicant must be fingerprinted electronically through L-1.

Non-Texas Residents must take the CHL course in the State of Texas and must undergo Texas background investigations to ensure they meet eligibility requirements.

Background checks include a search of the National Criminal Information Center (NCIC) database, and the Interstate Identification Index (IDI) maintained by the Federal Bureau of Investigations.

CHL Eligibility Requirements

Eligibility requirements for the CHL is covered in Texas Government Code §411.172 and §411.173. It's a good idea to understand these requirements prior to taking an approved CHL course. DPS will issue a CHL if the applicant meets the eligibility requirements listed below.

1. Must be a legal resident of the State of Texas or otherwise be eligible for a license as a non-resident under Section 411.173(a) (Non Resident License).

There is no longer a 6 month residency requirement to apply. If the applicant has moved to Texas, they may apply at any time. As of September 1, 2005 under House Bill 225 a legal resident of another state who meets the eligibility criteria other than residency may obtain a non-resident concealed handgun license. They must take the classes in the State of Texas and must undergo the same background checks as Texas residents.

2. Must be at least 21 years of age. A person under the age of 21 may take the proficiency course; but must be 21 before submitting an application to DPS. Active military personnel 18 to 20 years of age are eligible under Texas GC Section 411.172(g) (military exception). A person who is at least 18 years of age is eligible for a license to carry a concealed handgun if the person:

- Is an active member or veteran of the U.S. armed forces, Reserves, or National Guard;
- Or was discharged under honorable conditions, and;
- Meets the other eligibility requirements except for the minimum age required by federal law to purchase a handgun. The issuance of a CHL to a person eligible under the military exception does not affect the person's ability to purchase a handgun or ammunition from a Federal Firearms Dealer. A person still must be at least 21 to purchase a handgun or ammunition. (See Active Military Section for more info on this topic).

3. Must not have been convicted of a felony (As 'convicted' is defined in Section 411.171 (4)).

A felony conviction makes an individual ineligible for a concealed handgun license. A person with deferred adjudication probation for a felony offense under Title 5 offenses or a Chapter 29 Penal Code offense is still not eligible.

Convicted means an adjudication of guilt or, except as provided in Section 411.1711, an order of deferred adjudication entered against a person by a court of competent jurisdiction whether or not the imposition of the sentence is subsequently probated and the person is discharged from community supervision.

The term does not include an adjudication of guilt or an order of deferred adjudication that has been subsequently:

- expunged;
- (B) pardoned under the authority of a state or federal official; or
- (C) otherwise vacated, set aside, annulled, invalidated, voided, or sealed under any state or federal law (effective Sept 1, 2009)

Texas Senate Bill 1424 amends the definitions section of the statute § 411.1711, to exclude convictions that have been "vacated, set-aside, annulled, invalidated, voided, or sealed".

It also amends the provisions of the statute that construe an offense as a felony if it is so classified "at the time of application", to instead require that the classification be determined by law "at the time it is committed", unless, at the time of application, the classification has been reduced from a felony to a misdemeanor.

Finally, it amends the Penal Code section governing "felons in possession" of prohibited weapons, by requiring that the classification of the offense be based on the law at the time of possession.

Under § 411.1711 A person is not convicted, as that term is defined by §411.1711, if an order of deferred adjudication was entered against the person on a date not less than 10 years preceding the date of the person's application for a license under this subchapter unless the order of deferred adjudication was entered against the person for an offense under Title 5, Penal Code, or Chapter 29, Penal Code Section 25.07, Penal Code or Section 30.02(c)(2) or (d) Penal Code.

All individuals must list any arrest or conviction information on the application. A dismissal or conviction set aside is not an expunction.

Here is a list of Title 5 disqualifying offenses:

Title 5 Penal Code (Offenses against the person)
Ch.19 Criminal Homicide

Sec. 19.01 Types of Criminal Homicide
Sec. 19.02 Murder
Sec. 19.03 Capital Murder
Sec. 19.04 Manslaughter
Sec. 19.05 Criminally Negligent Homicide
Sec. 119.06 Applicability to Certain Conduct (death of an unborn child)

Ch. 20 Kidnapping and Unlawful Restraint
Sec. 20.01 Definitions
Sec. 20.02 Unlawful Restraint
Sec. 20.03 Kidnapping
Sec. 20.04 Aggravated Kidnapping
Sec. 20.05 Unlawful Transport

Ch. 20A Trafficking of Persons
Sec. 20A.01 Definitions
Sec. 20A.02 Trafficking of Persons

Ch. 21 Sexual Offenses
Sec. 21.01 Definitions
Sec. 21.02 Continuous Sexual Abuse of Young Child or Children
Sec. 21.06 Homosexual Conduct (ruled unconstitutional by U.S. Supreme Court)
Sec. 21.07 Public Lewdness
Sec. 21.08 Indecent Exposure
Sec. 21.11 Indecency with a Child
Sec. 21.12 Improper Relationship between Educator and Student
Sec. 21.15 Improper Photography or Visual Recording

Ch. 22 Assaultive Offenses
Sec. 22.01 Assault
Sec. 22.011 Sexual Assault
Sec. 22.015 Coercing Soliciting, or Inducing Gang Membership
Sec. 22.02 Aggravated Assault
Sec. 22.021 Aggravated Sexual Assault
Sec. 22.04 Injury to a Child, Elderly Individual or Disabled Individual
Sec. 22.041 Abandoning or Endangering Child
Sec. 22/05 Deadly Conduct

Sec. 25.07 Violation of Protective Order or Magistrate's Order

Ch 29 Robbery
Sec. 29.01 Definitions
Sec. 29.02 Robbery
Sec. 29.03 Aggravated Robbery
Sec. 30.02 Burglary (c) (2) or (d) Habitation.

4. Must not be currently charged in any jurisdiction with the commission of a Class A or Class B misdemeanor or equivalent level offense, or an offense under Section 42.01 of the Texas Penal Code (Disorderly Conduct) or equivalent offense or of a felony under an information or indictment.

A person who has charges pending is not eligible for a concealed handgun License. They should wait to apply until the charges are dismissed, assuming they are otherwise eligible at the time.

5. Must not be a fugitive from justice for a felony or Class A or Class B misdemeanor or equivalent offense in any jurisdiction'.

This could apply to a person who skipped a court date or to a person who has failed to comply with the terms of a court order.

6. Must not be a chemically dependent.

A "chemically dependent person" means a person who frequently or repeatedly becomes intoxicated by excessive indulgence in alcohol or uses controlled substances or dangerous drugs so as to acquire a fixed habit and an involuntary tendency to become intoxicated or use those substances as often as the opportunity is presented. (As defined in Section 411.171 (2).

A person with two convictions within the ten year period preceding the date of application for offenses (Class B or greater) involving the use of alcohol or a controlled substance may be considered ineligible as a chemically dependent person. Other evidence of chemical dependency may also make an individual ineligible for a CHL.

7. Must not be incapable of exercising sound judgment with respect to the proper use and storage of a handgun.

In accordance with Texas GC §411.172 if an applicant has been diagnosed by a licensed physician as suffering from a psychiatric disorder or condition that causes or is likely to cause substantial impairment in judgment, mood, perception, impulse control or intellectual ability. Suffers from a psychiatric disorder or condition that is in remission but is reasonably likely to redevelop at a future time; or requires continuous medical treatment to avoid redevelopment; has been diagnosed by a licensed physician, determined by a review board or similar authority, or declared by a court to be incompetent to manage the person's own affairs; or has entered in a criminal proceeding a plea of not guilty by reason of insanity.

Just because there was a diagnosis does not necessarily make them ineligible, but applicants need to inform DPS. The Medical Advisory Board will then receive the application and make the determination.

If an applicant has a psychiatric disorder or condition which may make an individual ineligible for a license, the application will be sent to the Medical Advisory Board (MAB) to determine whether the applicant is eligible to receive a license. Section 411.172(d) lists the guidelines used by MAB.

It would be a good idea for an applicant to show these guidelines to a treating physician before applying for a license. A person may also be ineligible due to involuntary commitment to a mental hospital.

8. Must not have been convicted in any jurisdiction of a Class A or Class B misdemeanor or equivalent offense or an offense under Section 42.01 Texas Penal Code (Disorderly Conduct), or equivalent offense. (as 'Convicted' is defined in Section 411.171(4), within the five years preceding the date of application.

The date of conviction (that is, the date the judge signed an order), not the date of arrest is used to determine whether a person's five year period has expired.

A conviction may occur several years after the date of arrest.
(Remember that conviction includes probation and deferred adjudication for purposes of eligibility).

If the applicant served any probation or paid a fine, they were probably convicted as defined by Section 411.171(4) of the statute.

9. Must be fully qualified under applicable federal and state laws to purchase a handgun.

Let's take a look at some of the federal prohibitors:

Federal Prohibitors

The "Brady" Law includes several eligibility requirements for purchasing a handgun. (Refer to Title 18 United States Code (U.S.C.) Section 922(g) (1) through (9) and (n)). A person with a dishonorable discharge or a conviction involving a misdemeanor crime of domestic violence, for example, is disqualified under the Brady Law from purchasing a handgun and is, therefore, not eligible for a CHL. Even a Class C simple assault can make an individual ineligible for a license under the provisions of the Brady law.

Let's take a look at some of these federal prohibitors:

- **Persons who have been convicted in any court of a crime punishable by imprisonment for a term exceeding one year, or**
- **Any state offence classified by the laws of the state as a misdemeanor and punishable by imprisonment for more than two years.**

What constitutes a conviction?   The judgment of a court, based on the verdict of a jury, or judicial officer, or on a plea of guilty or nolo contender of the defendant. Ref: 18 U.S.C. Section 922 (g) (1)

<u>Other things to consider are</u>:
- o   The prison sentence that could have been received.
- o   The actual disposition of the case.
- o   What state law requires for a conviction.

It is important for applicants with any type of assault arrest to make sure they are eligible to purchase under federal law before applying. It's also important for CHL Instructors to see what actually happened if they attempt to try to answer student questions about eligibility because an instructor cannot always provide an informed answer to a question without knowing whether a student was actually convicted and if so, of what type/class of crime etc. Ref: 18 U.S.C. Section 922 (g) (1).

- **Fugitives from justice.** Persons who are fugitives from justice as those who has:
    - Fled from any state to avoid prosecution from a felony or misdemeanor; or
    - A person who leaves the state to avoid giving testimony in any criminal proceeding; or
    - A person who knows felony or misdemeanor charges are pending against such person and leaves the state of prosecution.

- **Any person who is subject to an active warrant.** Ref: 18 U.S.C. Section 922 (g) (2).

- **Persons who are unlawful users of or addicted to any controlled substance**

The term "controlled substance" includes, but is not limited to, marijuana, depressants, stimulants, and narcotic drugs. The term does not include distilled spirits, wine, malt beverages, tobacco, or huffing.

Persons who are unlawful users of or addicted to any controlled substance are defined as: persons who use a controlled substance and have lost the power of self-control with reference to the use of the controlled substance; or persons who are current users of a controlled substance in a manner other than prescribed by a license physician.

- **Unlawful possession of a controlled substance.**
    Examples:
    - A person convicted for use or possession of a controlled substance within the past year; or
    - A person with multiple arrests for use of possession of a controlled substance within the past five years if the most recent arrest occurred within the past year; or
    - Admission of recent use or possession; or
    - A positive field or lab test will support this prohibitor, provided the test was administered within the past year.
        - Drug test during probation
        - Field test during an arrest

    Time starts from the date of the arrest, or the date of conviction within the past year. Evidence of possession could constitute a prohibitor even though the individual is actually convicted of a different or lesser offense.
    Ref: 18 U.S.C. Section 922 (g) (3).

- **Person who have been adjudicated as mental defectives or committed to a mental institution.** Adjudicated as a mental defective is a determination made by a court, board, commission, or other lawful authority that a person, as a result of marked subnormal

intelligence, mental illness, incompetency, condition, or disease:
- o Is a danger to himself or others; or
- o Lacks the mental capacity to contract or manage their own affairs, or
- o Is found to be insane by a court in a criminal case; or
- o Is found incompetent to stand trial or found not guilty by reason of insanity or lack of mental responsibility pursuant to the Uniform Code of Military Justice.

Adjudicated as a Mental Defective does not include merely being diagnosed of mental illness or disease. When a person has been formally committed to a mental institution by a court, board, commission, or other lawful authority this includes a commitment:
- o To a mental institution involuntarily; and
- o For mental defectiveness or mental illness; or
- o For other reasons, such as for drug use.

The term "Mental Institution" includes any health facility that provides diagnoses by a licensed professional of mental illness or retardation, including a general hospital.

Qualifying commitments must be involuntary and must be for treatment. Qualifying commitments does not include voluntary admissions or commitments for evaluation/observation.

Ref: 18 U.S.C. Section 922 (g) (4)

- **Person who are aliens and are illegally or unlawfully in the United States.** Only a legal and lawful alien can purchase or redeem a firearm.

    Examples of illegal/unlawful aliens:
    - An alien who unlawfully entered the United Sates without inspection and authorization by an immigration officer or who has not been paroled.
    - A nonimmigrant whose authorized period of stay has expired or how has violated the terms of the nonimmigrant category.
    - An alien under an order of deportation, exclusion, or removal or under an order to depart the United States Voluntarily.
    - An alien who is an applicant for asylum.

An Immigrant Alien is any alien who has been lawfully admitted for permanent residence and has been afforded the privilege of residing permanently in the United States.

A Non-Immigrant Alien is any alien having a residence in a foreign country which he/she has no intention of abandoning for example:
- Admitted for a temporary period of time.
- Admitted for a specific purpose.

    Ref: 18 U.S.C. Section 922 (g) (5)

- **Persons who have been discharged from the U.S. Armed Forces under dishonorable conditions.** A person whose separation from the U.S. Armed Forces resulted from:
    o A dishonorable discharge, or
    o A dismissal.
  Ref: 18 U.S.C. Section 922 (g) (6)

- **Persons who, having been citizens of the United States, have renounced their citizenship.** Ref: 18 U.S.C. Section 922 (g)(7)
- **Persons subject to a court order that restrains them from harassing, stalking, or threatening an intimate partner or child of such intimate partner, or from engaging in other conduct that would place the intimate partner or child in reasonable fear of bodily injury.** There are four criteria for the federal prohibition. I have listed the four criteria from the letters A thru D as follows:
  A. Hearing:
     o The order was issued after a hearing of which actual notice was given to the person and at which the person had an opportunity to participate.
  B. Intimate Partner:
     o The protected person must be:
        i. A spouse or former spouse of the respondent

  ii. A parent of a child in common with the respondent
  iii. An individual who cohabitates or has cohabitated with the respondent
  iv. A child of the respondent
  v. A child of an intimate partner of the respondent

C. <u>Restrains Future Conduct:</u>
- The order restrains defendant/respondent from harassing, stalking, or threatening the intimate partner or child of such intimate partner; or
- The order restrains defendant/respondent from engaging in other conduct that would place the intimate partner in reasonable fear of bodily injury to the partner or child.

D. <u>Credible Threat or Physical Force:</u>
- The order includes a finding that defendant/respondent is a credible threat to the physical safety of the intimate partner or child; or
- The order, by its terms, explicitly prohibits the use, attempted use, or threatened use of physical force against the intimate partner or child

that would reasonably be expected to cause bodily injury.

The protective order may stipulate that the subject is prohibited from possessing firearms. If this is the case, then he/she is ineligible under federal law to possess firearms. Ref: 18 U.S.C. Section 922 (g) (8)

- **Persons convicted in any court of a misdemeanor crime of domestic violence (MCDV).**

    <u>Conviction Level</u>:
    - If a misdemeanor under local, state, tribal, or federal law; or
    - In states which do not classify offenses as misdemeanors, is an offense which is punishable by imprisonment for a term of one year or less, and includes offenses that are punishable by a fine.

    <u>Conviction Relationship</u>:
    - Was committed by a current or former spouse, or parent, or guardian of the victim; or
    - By a person with whom the victim shares a child in common; or
    - By a person who is cohabitating with or has cohabitated with the victim as a spouse, parent, or guardian; or

- By a person who is or has been similarly situated to a spouse, parent, or guardian of the victim.
- Has as an element, the use or attempted use of physical force (e.g., assault, battery, disorderly conduct); or the threatened use of a deadly weapon.

Ref: 18 U.S.C. Section 922 (g) (9)

Persons who are under indictment or information in any court for a crime punishable by imprisonment for a term exceeding one year. Ref: 18 U.S.C. Section 922 (n)

10. Must not have been finally determined to be delinquent in making child support payments administered or collected by the Attorney General.

A person must clear up any delinquency in paying court-ordered child support before applying for a CHL.

11. Must not have been finally determined to be delinquent in the payment of taxes or other money collected by the comptroller, state treasurer, or tax collector of any agency or political subdivision of this state (or state of residence for non-resident applicants).

A person must clear up any tax delinquencies before applying for a CHL.

12. Must not be currently restricted under a court protective order or subject to a restraining order affecting the spousal relationship, not including a restraining orders affecting only property.

If a person's spouse or ex-spouse has a protective or restraining order against the person, even an agreed order, then the applicant must wait until the order expires before applying for a CHL.

13. Must not in the past 10 years been adjudicated as having engaged in delinquent conduct violating a penal law of the grade of felony.

This section applies only to Juvenile offenses, not to felonies committed by adults. Juveniles are not convicted, unless certified as an adult.

They are adjudicated as having engaged in delinquent conduct. For example, if a person was adjudicated to be a juvenile delinquent at the age of 16 for the commission of a felony, they are not eligible for a CHL until they turn 26 years of age.

Texas law allows juvenile records to be unsealed for purposes of determining whether a person is eligible under this section. So, even if the offense was a juvenile offense, the applicant must list it on the application to apply for a CHL.

14. You must not have made any material misrepresentation, or failed to disclose any material fact in an application.

If a person fails to include information on an application or request that was required to be listed, he is not eligible for a license and the application will be denied, or the license will be revoked if DPS discover the misrepresentation after it has been issued.

A person should pay close attention to the fourteen eligibility requirements before applying for the Texas CHL because the application license fees that are paid to DPS are not refundable.

Legal Resident Alien

During the CHL course a question most often asked is can legal resident aliens get a Texas CHL.? Under federal law, aliens who have been admitted to the U.S. under a non-immigrant visa, usually are not qualified to purchase a handgun and therefore, do not qualify for a license. However, as long as you were not admitted under a non-immigrant visa and are a legal resident of Texas, you may qualify.

I recommend that if you fall under this category you should contact DPS for the official answer.

The CHL Application Process

Most CHL Instructors will assist you with ensuring that you have all the necessary documentation needed to submit to the Texas Department of Public Safety. If possible ensure that you have already completed your CHL application online through the DPS website and have the checklist of documents in hand when you attend the CHL course. If you download the forms yourself, make sure that you have all the required documents.

(**Note:** you may need additional paperwork if you apply under a special condition).

An applicant for a license to carry a concealed handgun must submit the following:

1. **A completed application (Form CHL-78A)**
   The application consists of:
   - Full name and place of birth;
   - Race and sex;
   - Residence and business addresses for the preceding five years;
   - Hair and eye color;
   - Height and weight;
   - Driver's license number or identification certificate number issued by DPS
   - Criminal history record information

    o History, if any of treatment (drug or alcohol or psychiatric hospital information.
2. **Two passport type photographs**
3. **A certified copy of the applicant's birth certificate or certified proof of age**; (A driver's license or states ID card may be acceptable)
4. **Proof of residency in the state**
5. **Electronic fingerprints** (through L-1 Enrollment Services)
6. **A non-refundable application and license fee paid directly to Texas DPS**
7. **Evidence of handgun proficiency** (Form CHL-100) issued by an approved Texas CHL course;
8. **Affidavits (not needed if applying online)** signed by you and notarized stating that you:
    a. (Form CHL-86)Have read and understands each provision of the Texas Concealed Handgun-Licensing Act (Texas Government Code Chapter 411, Subchapter H) that creates an offense under the laws of the State and each provision of the laws of the state related to use of deadly force and fulfill all the eligibility requirements listed under Section 411.172; and;
    b. (Form CHL-85) which authorize the release of information and records to DPS to conduct a background investigation 411.174(a) (9).

Once you have completed all the required paperwork and CHL course you can now submit all of your documents to DPS. The preferred method is to complete your application online through the DPS website prior to taking a CHL course. By doing this, notarized affidavits are no longer needed. In addition, by applying online this will ensure that you are entered into the CHL database which allows you the ability to get fingerprinted using the L-1 Enrollment Services electronically. Electronic capture and submission of fingerprints routinely results in a 24-48 hour completion of the criminal history check process (including the FBI check).

Prints captured digitally on L-1's industry leading "Live scan" systems reject at or below the FBI's average of 2% compared with 10-30% for traditional ink card processing. Lower reject rates means less frustration and wasted time for CHL applicants. Once you have submitted your application via online with DPS you can now schedule a fingerprint appointment through the DPS website or visit the L-1 website directly at www.L-1enrollment.com or by calling 888-467-2080. The fee for fingerprinting is currently set at $9.95.

The Texas CHL Certification Course

The CHL course consists of three parts: the classroom Power Point Slide presentation, the final exam that consist of 50 multiple choice and True/False questions and finally the handgun proficiency demonstration. An applicant cannot take the CHL course at the Texas DPS. DPS only provides training for instructors. The CHL instructor list found on the DPS website is a list of Certified Instructors that have given DPS permission to post their contact information for the public. The DPS will not release information about any instructor or applicant except for criminal justice purposes.

The Texas CHL course is not a "how to shoot" course so applicants will need to know how to operate their handgun safely prior to attending the course. The law does not require classes to be offered in any language other than English. However, classes may be offered in other languages as long as instructors teach key English phrases such as "I have a handgun" and "May I see your concealed handgun license?"

In accordance with Texas Government Code §411.188 only a qualified Handgun Instructor approved by DPS may administer a handgun proficiency course. The DPS director, by rule, shall establish minimum standards for handgun proficiency and shall develop a course to teach handgun proficiency and examinations to measure proficiency. The course to teach handgun proficiency must contain training sessions divided into two parts.

One part of the course must be classroom instruction and the other part must be range instruction and an actual demonstration by the applicant on the applicant's ability to safely and proficiently use the applicable category of handgun in which they are to be licensed.

An applicant must be able to demonstrate, at a minimum, the degree of proficiency that is required to effectively operate a handgun of at least a .32 caliber or above.

If the applicant qualified on the range with a semi-automatic handgun, their license will have the category "SA" (Semi-Automatic). If you qualify with the SA category you will be allowed to carry either a revolver or semi-auto of any caliber.

If a person qualified on the range with a revolver, their license will have the category of "NSA" (not Semi-Automatic) and <u>will be only licensed to carry a revolver.</u>

<u>To legally carry both a semi-automatic and/or a revolver, an applicant must qualify with a semi-automatic.</u> DPS distributes the standards, course requirements, and examinations to qualified handgun instructors.

Some instructors may require the applicant to use their own gun during the firing range portion of the course. However, others may provide guns for the applicants to use. The CHL issued by the Texas DPS is not associated with a specific gun. However, the license is specific to the type of gun action (i.e. semi=automatic or non-semi-automatic).

The CHL course must include at least 10 hours and not more than 15 hours of instruction on the following subjects at a minimum:

- The laws that relate to weapons and to the use of deadly force;
- Handgun use, proficiency, and safety;
- Nonviolent dispute resolution; and
- Proper storage practices for handguns with an emphasis on storage practices that eliminate the possibility of accidental injury to a child.

CHL instructors are not authorized to waive any training proficiency requirements.

Applicants must also take a proficiency examination at the end of the CHL course. Only a qualified handgun instructor may administer the examination.

The proficiency examination must include:

- A written test on the subjects taught in the 10 to 15 hour CHL course; and
- A physical demonstration of proficiency in the use of one or more handguns of specific categories and in handgun safety procedures.

The written examination currently consists of 50 questions in the form of multiple choice and true and false questions. The applicant will complete the exam at the end of the CHL course and must score at least 70% to pass.

To successfully qualify with the handgun, shooters must complete the handgun proficiency with a minimum score of 70% (175 out of a possible 250 points).

The physical demonstration of proficiency with a handgun consists of firing 50 rounds of ammunition into a B-27 target. The B-27 target used for the CHL handgun qualification course is a human-shaped silhouette target measuring 45 inches by 24 inches and come in one of the four different colors of Black, Red, Green or Blue.

The minimum caliber of handgun to qualify during the handgun proficiency demonstration must be at least .32 caliber (9mm and .380 are acceptable). A person cannot qualify with anything smaller and laser sights are not permitted.

The course of fire is timed. The B-27 target has scoring rings of 5, 4 & 3 respectively. The target will be scored utilizing the scoring diagram in the upper left hand corner of the target. If you hit in the 8, 9 or X rings you will receive 5 points. The 7th ring is worth 4 points and if your rounds hit anywhere on the target but outside the rings you will receive 3 points. Your points must total at least 175 to pass.

Under supervised instruction at the CHL course an applicant will fire three stages:

Stage 1:

- **20 rounds from the 3 yard line**
    - 1 shot fired in 2 seconds, (5 times)
    - 2 shots fired in 3 seconds, (5 times)
    - 5 shots fired in 10 seconds, (1 time only)

Stage 2:
- **20 rounds from the 7 yard line**
    - 5 shots fired in 10 seconds, (1 time only)

- 2 shots fired in 4 seconds, (1time)
- 3 shots fired in 6 seconds, (1time)
- 1 shot fired in 3 seconds, (5 times)
- 5 shots fired in 15 seconds, (1time only)

Stage 3:
- **10 rounds from the 15 yard line**
  - 2 shots fired in 6 seconds, (1time)
  - 3 shots fired in 9 seconds, (1time)
  - 5 shots fired in 15 seconds, (1time)

All firing stages will be controlled by the Range Master/CHL instructor. If any malfunctions are encountered, the shooter will work through the problem and finish the course of fire.

A shot fired late deducts points and if an applicant has a malfunction and does not fire a shot during the firing string, the shot cannot be made up. Just as in the real world. An applicant should practice firing the handgun they will use prior to attending the CHL course. The Applicants must know how to safely operate their handgun.

Unsafe handling, accidental discharge or firing out of sequence during the course may be grounds for dismissal or disqualification. The applicant will be given three attempts to pass the shooting proficiency. Make-up opportunities to re- shoot the course are at the instructor's discretion. It is recommended that applicants that have never fired a handgun take a basic handgun course prior to taking the Texas CHL course.

What does "qualified" mean? In my opinion it means a person does not need help completing a task as they possess all the skills required. It's a big responsibility to carry a concealed handgun and CHL Instructors will not certify an applicant if they cannot show that they can operate their handgun safely and do not pass the handgun proficiency shooting practical.

It's a good idea to find a gun range that you are comfortable with and practice with your handgun of choice prior to taking a CHL course. This will ensure that you will have no issues when it's time to qualify. There are multiple ranges located around the Great State of Texas to choose from.

The Texas CHL Academy in San Antonio also offers basic shooting courses for those individuals who may not have ever handled a handgun or who would like to gain confidence in knowing handgun basics.

DPS can and does monitor classes or training presented by qualified CHL instructors. Qualified instructors may not and are not allowed to waive any proficiency requirements of applicants who they know may be proficient. Qualified instructors must follow the rules established by DPS.

Throughout the State of Texas, CHL Instructors pride themselves on their ability to provide quality instruction.

The common goal is to ensure that all applicants wishing to obtain a Texas CHL are knowledgeable of the laws of

Texas as they pertain to concealed carry and are proficient with their ability to safely handle, operate and store their handguns from unauthorized persons.

CHL courses offered throughout the state vary in price. DPS does not regulate what price instructors charge for their service. A cheaper price does not always mean quality, so shop around. Be sure to find an experienced instructor with a passion for what they do. I recommend the Texas Concealed Handgun Academy located in San Antonio, TX. The website is www.TexasCHLacademy.com.

A qualified handgun instructor may submit to DPS, a written recommendation for disapproval of the application for a CHL license, renewal, or modification of a license, accompanied by an affidavit stating personal knowledge or naming persons with personal knowledge of facts that lead the instructor to believe that an applicant does not possess the required handgun proficiency.

DPS may use a written recommendation submitted by an instructor as the basis for denial of a license only if DPS determines that the recommendation is made in good faith and is supported by a preponderance of the evidence. DPS will make a determination not later than the 45th day after the date DPS receives the written recommendation. You can read more about this topic in the Texas GC§411.188.

Once you have completed the CHL course you are now able to submit all required documents to DPS. The certification (CHL-100) provided by the CHL Instructor is valid for up to two years.

This means that you can submit your paperwork up to DPS the same day, or the next year, but you must submit it before the two year date or re-take the CHL course. The address to send your packet to <u>if not including payment</u> is:

Concealed Handgun Licensing Bureau
Regulatory Licensing Service MSC 0245
Texas Department of Public Safety
PO Box 4087
Austin, Texas 78773-0245

On receipt of your CHL packet by DPS at its Austin Headquarters, the department will conduct the appropriate criminal history records check of the applicant. No later than the 30th day after the date the department receives the application materials; DPS will forward the materials to the director's designee in the geographical area of the applicant's residence to conduct the investigation. The director's designee as needed will conduct an additional criminal history record check of the applicant and an investigation of the applicant's local official records to verify the accuracy of the application materials. No later than the 60th day after DPS received the application material the investigation must be completed. DPS will send a fingerprint card to the

Federal Bureau of Investigation for a national criminal history check of the applicant.

On completion of the investigation, all materials and the results of the investigation will be returned to the appropriate division of DPS at its Austin headquarters. DPS will conduct any further record check or investigation that DPS determines is necessary if a question exists with respect to the accuracy of the application materials or the eligibility of the applicant. This process could take up to 180 days.

DPS will administer the licensing procedures in good faith so that any applicant who meets all the eligibility requirements and submits all the application materials shall receive a license. DPS will not deny an application on the basis of a capricious or arbitrary decision made by the department.

DPS will no later than the 60th day after the date of the receipt by the director's designee of the completed application materials:

- Issue the license;
- Notify the applicant in writing that the application was denied:
    - On the grounds that the applicant failed to qualify under the criteria listed in Section 411.172;

- o Based on the affidavit of the director's designee submitted to the department under Section 411.176(c); or
- o Based on the affidavit of the qualified handgun instructor submitted to DPS under Section 411.188(k); or
- o Notify the applicant in writing that the department is unable to make a determination regarding the issuance or denial of a license to the applicant within the 60-day period prescribed and include in that notification an explanation of the reason for the inability and an estimation of the amount of time the department will need to make the determination.

Failure of the department to issue or deny a license for a period of more than 30 days after DPS is required to act constitutes denial. For more information on the topic of denial, review Texas GC§411.177.

If the background investigation is complete a decision will be made for approval or disapproval. If approved, DPS will issue and send the CHL to the applicant through the mail to the address listed on the application.

Information on individuals who are licensed to carry a concealed handgun is confidential and not subject to requests under the Public Information Act. However, DPS may release information about a concealed handgun licensee to criminal justice agencies.

DPS shall disclose to criminal justice agency information contained in its files and records regarding whether a named individual or any individual named in specified list is licensed. The information on an individual subject to disclosure includes the individual's name, date of birth, gender, race, and zip code, telephone number, e-mail address, and internet website address. Except as otherwise provided by Section 411.192 and by Section 411.193, all other records maintained are confidential and are not subject to mandatory disclosure under the open records law, Chapter 552.

An applicant or CHL holder may be furnished a copy of disclosable records regarding the applicant or CHL holder on request and the payment of a reasonable fee. DPS shall notify a license holder of any request that is made for information relating to the license holder under this section and provide the name of the agency making the request.

General information about the Concealed Handgun Statue

Confidentiality of Records

Texas House Bill 991 Confidentiality of Records makes confidential, information that was previously disclosed to the public regarding whether a named individual is licensed to carry a concealed handgun, and the licensee's name, date of birth, gender, race and zip code. Subsequent changes in 2009 added telephone number, email address, and internet website address. Texas DPS shall disclose information to a criminal justice agency.

In accordance with Texas GC §411.192. Confidentiality of Records:

(a) The department shall disclose to criminal justice agency information contained in its files and records regarding whether a named individual or any individual named in a specified list is licensed under this subchapter. Information on an individual's name, date of birth, gender, race, zip code, telephone number, e-mail address, and internet website address. Except as otherwise provided by this section and by Section 411.193, all other records maintained under this subchapter are confidential and are not subject to mandatory disclosure under the open records law, Chapter 552.

(b) An applicant or license holder may be furnished a copy of dis-closable records regarding the applicant or license holder on request and the payment of a reasonable fee.

(c) The department shall notify a license holder of any request that is made for information relating to the license holder under this section and provide the name of the agency making the request.

Ref: Texas GC §411.192

Change of Address or Name

If a CHL holder has a change of address or name by marriage or otherwise, or status becomes inapplicable for purposes of the information required to be displayed on the license, The CHL holder <u>must notify DPS within 30 days</u> of the change. The CHL holder must also pay the fee of $25 for a duplicate license. You may download the forms needed for name and address changes or status changes from the downloadable forms section located on the DPS website.

If a CHL holder fails to properly notify DPS of a name or address change can result in a 30 day suspension of the CHL.

It is important for license holders to submit change of address forms as soon as possible, because all notices under the statue are sent by certified mail to the last reported address.

If the certified mail is returned to DPS as undeliverable, the statute requires notice to be given by publication once in a paper of general interest in the county of the last reported address. If DPS gives notice of an action by publication, the action takes effect on the 31st day after the notice was published. In other words, a license may be suspended or revoked without actual knowledge if the CHL holder fails to notify DPS of a change of address.

If you are a college student and a resident of the State of Texas and you are merely attending a university in another state, you may keep your permanent address on your concealed handgun license. If after you graduate from the university or you move out of your parent's home, then follow the procedure for requesting a duplicate license with the address change including paying the appropriate fee.

You may change your address online at: www.txdps.state.tx.us or you may download a Request for Duplicate Concealed Handgun License and Change of Name or Address form, under the downloadable forms link on the CHL website. You may also send a letter including your full name, CHL number, old address and new address and a cashier's check, money order or personal check for $25 to the Texas Department of Public Safety, Concealed Handgun Licensing Bureau, P.O. Box 15888, Austin, Texas, 78761-5888.

> Ref: Texas GC §411.181

Modification of the CHL

The categories of handguns are:
1. SA: semi-automatic and
2. NSA: handguns that are not semi-automatic (revolver).

A person licensed under "SA" <u>will be allowed to carry any type of handgun.</u> However, a person licensed under "NSA" will only be licensed to carry a "NSA". If a person has a "NSA" designation on their CHL and wish to change to a "SA" a person has to modify a license to allow a CHL holder to carry a handgun of a different category than the license indicates. To do so, a CHL holder must:

- Complete a proficiency examination (A new CHL-100 with "SA" designation) as provided by Section 411.188(e); and submit an application for a modified license (CHL-70 downloadable forms)
- Include two recent color passport type photos
- A signed photo holder (CHL-6)

The fee to modify is determined by DPS and is currently set at: $25. Senior Citizen, Indigent and Veterans fees are $12.50. The fee for a Felony Prosecuting Attorney and Active Military are waived. On receipt of a modified license, the CHL holder <u>shall return the previously issued license back to DPS.</u> Failure to do so, the CHL holder is at risk for suspension of the CHL.

Ref: Texas GC 411.184

Length of the CHL License

An original CHL expires on the first birthday of the license holder after the fourth anniversary of the date of issuance. For example, a license holder has a birth date of 10/15/51. The license is issued on 4/18/07 and the fourth anniversary of the date of issuance is 4/18/11. The license will expire on the next birthday, 10/15/11. The expiration date of the CHL can be found on the front of the license colored in red.

When it is time for renewal the renewed licenses are effective for 5 years. After the third renewal the CHL is good for a 10 year period. Check with DPS to see when the 10 year period starts for your particular license.

Concealed Handgun License Renewal

If a CHL holder wishes to renew the Texas CHL, they must take a 4 to 6 hours continuing education course in handgun proficiency under Section 411.188 (c) not more than the six-months before applying for renewal. After completion of the renewal course the Form CHL-100 provided by the CHL Instructor is valid for 6 months.

The renewal course consists of the use of deadly force and places where it is unlawful for a CHL holder to carry a concealed handgun, other related laws and other instructor topics applicable. You must also re-qualify with the handgun.

Fingerprints and color photos are not required to be submitted for renewal of the CHL at this time however DPS may request these items if they become unreadable from previous submissions or any other reason that they deem necessary.

In certain circumstances, a person may be exempt from taking the renewal course. If you have been continuously licensed for three (3) renewal periods, you should contact the Concealed

In accordance with Texas GC§411.185(A) to renew a license, a CHL holder must:

(1) complete a continuing education course in handgun proficiency under Section 411.188(c) within the six month period preceding the date of application for renewal, for a first or second renewal, and the date of application for renewal, or the date of application for the preceding renewal, for a third or subsequent renewal to ensure that the license holder is not required to complete the course more than once in any ten year period;

(2) submit evidence of proficiency under Section 411.189 within the six month period preceding the date of application for renewal, for the first or second renewal; and (b) the date of application for renewal or the date of application for the preceding renewal, for a third or subsequent renewal to ensure that the license holder is not required to obtain the certificate more than once in any ten year period. (Note: this follows after the 1st and 2nd renewals).

Handgun Licensing Bureau at DPS to see if you are exempt from attending a CHL renewal course.

The law change was designed to allow those long time license holders to only need to take the class every ten years. If you qualify for the every ten year renewal class it is the CHL holder's responsibility for keeping current with any changes in the law.

DPS may offer online, or allow a qualified handgun instructor to offer online, the continuing education instruction course and written section of the proficiency examination required to renew a license in accordance with Texas GC§411.188(j).

In accordance with Texas GC§411.190(d-1) The department shall ensure that an applicant may renew certification under section (d) from any county in the state by using an online format to complete the required retraining course if: the applicant is renewing for the first time, or the applicant completed the retraining course in person the previous time the applicant renewed certification.

A license holder may renew a license up to one year after the license has expired. A CHL holder may not carry concealed if the license has expired. A CHL holder must have a valid CHL license in their possession to carry a concealed handgun on or about their person outside the confines of your home or vehicle. The exception to this is that the concealed handgun may be carried in your vehicle as long as you comply with the requirements of Section 46.02 of the Texas Penal Code (Unlawful Carrying of a Weapon).

After twelve months in which a CHL had expired and if the person did not renew their license, the CHL holder will be required to reapply as a new applicant and take the 10 to 15 hour course all over again.

The fee to renew a CHL was set at $70 at the time of publication of this guide. A CHL holder may be eligible for a reduced renewal fee under a special condition. Fees are set by DPS and are subject to change, so it is the responsibility of the CHL holder check the DPS website for current information prior to reapplying.

Rights of Employers

This subchapter does not prevent or otherwise limit the right of a public or private employer to prohibit persons who are licensed under this subchapter from carrying a concealed handgun on the premises of the business.

In this section, "premises" has the meaning assigned by Section 46.035(f) (3), Penal Code.

So in short, an employer may prohibit, but are not required to prohibit an employee who is a CHL holder from carrying on the job; but not from keeping a firearm in their privately owned vehicle in the employer's parking lot, unless the employer falls under one of the exemptions. A (30.06) sign is not required for employees and notice may be given during orientation or provided in a policy manual. If an individual received notice and carries anyway they may be charged with a Class A misdemeanor.

The last session of the Texas Legislature passed one significant Pro-gun bill. As of September 1st, 2011 <u>you may now keep your handgun locked in your motor vehicle in the parking lot of the employer.</u> Some people refer to this as the "parking Lot Law". Your employer may not forbid you from doing so. Be mindful that there are some exceptions so read Sec. 52.062 of the Labor Code "EXCEPTIONS". Also read Sec. 52.063. "IMMUNITY FROM CIVIL LIABILITY".

The passing of the bill amended Chapter 52 of the Labor Code by adding Subchapter G to read as follows:

SUBCHAPTER G. RESTRICTIONS ON PROHIBITING EMPLOYEE TRANSPORTATION OR STORAGE OF CERTAIN FIREARMS OR AMMUNITION

Sec.52.061. RESTRICTION ON PROHIBITING EMPLOYEE ACCESS TO OR STORAGE OF FIREARM OR AMMUNITION.

A public or private employer may not prohibit an employee who holds a license to carry a concealed handgun under Subchapter H, Chapter 411, Government Code, who otherwise lawfully possesses a firearm, or who lawfully possesses ammunition from transporting or storing a firearm or ammunition the employee is authorized by law to possess in a locked, privately owned motor vehicle in a parking lot, parking garage, or other parking area the employer provides for employees.

Sec. 52.062. EXCEPTIONS.

(a) Section 52.061 does not:

(1) authorize a person who holds a license to carry a concealed handgun under Subchapter H, Chapter 411, Government Code, who otherwise lawfully possesses a firearm, or who lawfully possesses ammunition to possess a firearm or ammunition on any property where the possession of a firearm or ammunition is prohibited by state or federal law; or

(2) Apply to:

(A) A vehicle owned or leased by a public or private employer and used by an employee in the course and scope of the employee's employment, unless the employee is required to transport or store a firearm in the official discharge of the employee's duties;

(B) A school district;

(C) An open-enrollment charter school, as defined by Section 5.001, Education Code;

(D) A private school, as defined by Section 22.081, Education Code;

(E) property owned or controlled by a person, other than the employer, that is subject to a valid, unexpired oil, gas, or other mineral lease that contains a provision prohibiting the possession of firearms on the property; or

(F) property owned or leased by a chemical manufacturer or oil and gas refiner with an air authorization under Chapter 382, Health and Safety Code, and on which the primary business conducted is the manufacture, use, storage, or transportation of hazardous, combustible, or explosive materials, except in regard to an employee who holds a license to carry a concealed handgun under Subchapter H, Chapter 411, Government Code, and who stores a firearm or ammunition the employee is authorized by law to possess in a locked, privately owned motor vehicle in a parking lot, parking garage, or other parking area the employer provides for employees that is outside of a secured and restricted area:

(i) That contains the physical plant;
(ii) that is not open to the public; and

(iii) The ingress into which is constantly monitored by security personnel.

(b) Section 52.061 does not prohibit an employer from prohibiting an employee who holds a license to carry a concealed handgun under Subchapter H, Chapter 411, Government Code, or who otherwise lawfully possesses a firearm, from possessing a firearm the employee is otherwise authorized by law to possess on the premises of the employer's business. In this subsection, "premises" has the meaning assigned by Section 46.035(f) (3), Penal Code.

Sec.52.063.IMMUNITY FROM CIVIL LIABILITY.

(a) Except in cases of gross negligence, a public or private employer, or the employer's principal, officer, director, employee, or agent, is not liable in a civil action for personal injury, death, property damage, or any other damages resulting from or arising out of an occurrence involving a firearm or ammunition that the employer is required to allow on the employer's property under this subchapter.

(b) The presence of a firearm or ammunition on an employer's property under the authority of this subchapter does not by itself constitute a failure by the employer to provide a safe workplace.

(c) For purposes of this section, a public or private employer, or the employer's principal, officer, director, employee, or agent, does not have a duty:

(1) To patrol, inspect, or secure:

(A) Any parking lot, parking garage, or other parking area the employer provides for employees; or

(B) any privately owned motor vehicle located in a parking lot, parking garage, or other parking area described by Paragraph (A); or

(2) To investigate, confirm, or determine an employee's compliance with laws related to the ownership or possession of a firearm or ammunition or the transportation and storage of a firearm or ammunition.

Ref: Texas GC§411.203

Displaying a Concealed Handgun License on a Peace Officer's Demand

If a CHL holder is carrying their handgun on or about their person and a peace officer or magistrate requests any type of identification from the person. The CHL holder <u>must show</u> both their driver's license or state issued identification <u>and</u> their Concealed Handgun License. If the CHL holder is not carrying a handgun on or about their person this requirement does not apply. This is a requirement under Texas GC§ 411.205.

So remember if you have your handgun on you and you get asked for any type of identification from a peace officer or magistrate you <u>are required</u> to show both, your identification and your CHL!

Ref: Texas GC§411.205

What to do during traffic stops

Traffic stop policies may vary among the different law enforcement agencies in the state. It is the CHL holder's responsibility to check with their local law enforcement agency to find out what the procedures are in the event of a traffic stop while carrying concealed. The most common practice is to:

1. Pull over as required.
2. Ensure that your driver's window is rolled down.
3. Shut off engine
4. Keep both hands in plain view and leaves them on the steering wheel. Do not make any sudden movements, especially towards the handgun.
5. Tell the officer that you have a concealed handgun license and are carrying your handgun as soon as possible.
6. At night turn on your vehicle's dome light.
7. Ask the officer "how would you like for me to proceed.
8. Follow the directions of the officer. Don't forget to show both, your driver's license and your CHL if asked for identification. (Note: You are required to display your CHL license).

Authority of Peace Officer to Disarm

In accordance with Texas GC§411.207:

(a) A peace officer who is acting in the lawful discharge of the officers official duties may disarm a license holder at any time the officer reasonably believes it is necessary for the protection of the license holder, officer, or another individual. The peace officer shall return the handgun to the license holder before discharging the license holder from the scene if the officer determines that the license holder is not a threat to the officer, license holder, or another individual and if the license holder has not violated any provision of this subchapter or committed any other violation that results in the arrest of the license holder.

(b) A peace officer who is acting in the lawful discharge of the officer's duties may temporarily disarm a license holder when a license holder enters a nonpublic, secure portion of a law enforcement facility, if the law enforcement agency provides a gun locker where the peace officer can secure the license holder's handgun. The peace officer shall secure the handgun in the locker and shall return the handgun to the license holder immediately after the license holder leaves the nonpublic, secure portion of the facility.

(c) A law enforcement facility shall prominently display at each entrance to a nonpublic, secure portion of the facility a sign that gives notice in both English and Spanish that, under this section, a peace officer may temporarily disarm a license holder when the license holders enters the nonpublic, secure portion of the facility. The sign must appear in contrasting colors with block letters at least one inch in height. The sign shall be displayed in a clearly visible and conspicuous manner.

(d) In this section:

(1) "Law enforcement facility" means a building or a portion of a building used exclusively by a law enforcement agency that employs peace officers as described by Articles 2.12(1) and (3), Code of Criminal Procedure, and support personnel to conduct the official business of the agency. The term does not include:

(a) Any portion of a building not actively used exclusively to conduct the official business of the agency; or

(b) Any public or private driveway, street, sidewalk, walkway, parking lot, parking garage, or other parking area.

(2) "Nonpublic, secure portion of a law enforcement facility" means that portion of a law enforcement facility to which the general public is denied access without express permission and to which access is granted solely to conduct the official business of the law enforcement agency.

Ref: Texas GC§411.207

Places where concealed handgun carry is not authorized in the State of Texas

It is important to know where you cannot take your concealed handgun in the State of Texas. Senate Bill 60 clearly provides that a license holder is not permitted to carry a concealed handgun in certain places. Section 46.03 of the Texas Penal Code specifically prohibits the carrying of a handgun (or other prohibited weapon) in certain places. An offense under section 46.03 is a third degree felony. These places include:

1. **On the physical premises of a public or private school or educational institution,** including passenger transportation vehicles of a school or education institution or on any grounds or building on which an activity sponsored by a school or education institution is being conducted.

2. **On the premises of a polling place on the day of election or while early voting is in progress**

3. **On the premises of any government court or offices used by the court,** unless pursuant to written regulations or written authorization of the court;

4. **On the premises of a racetrack**

5. **Into a secured area of an airport** or

6. **Within 1,000 feet of premises on a day that a sentence of death is set to be imposed** on the designated premises.

"**Secured area**" means an area of an airport terminal building to which access is controlled by the inspection of persons and property under federal law. If you wanted to take your handgun with you on a flight to another state in which the State of Texas has reciprocity you may be allowed to bring your handgun in a lockable case, unloaded with no ammunition to the ticket counter where you purchase airline tickets. It is your responsibility to contact the airlines directly to find out what are the specific requirements to transport a handgun if granted permission to do so on their aircraft.

Section 46.03 does not apply to: a district attorney, municipal attorney, or county attorney who is licensed to carry; or a bailiff designated by an active judicial officer who is licensed to carry and engaged in escorting the judicial officer; or to an assistant district attorney, assistant criminal district attorney, or an assistant county attorney who are licensed to carry. Texas House Bill 2300 created unique concealed handgun licenses for Certain judges and prosecutors and providing exemptions from certain unlawful carrying provisions. The house bill adopted:

- Procedures to indicate the status on the license

- Exempts them of places prohibited to carry concealed

- Exempts them from the handgun proficiency certificate, if a Texas Commission on Law Enforcement Officer Standards and Education (TCLEOSE) instructor certifies their proficiency (within one year)

- Texas House Bill 1889 addresses some similar points for prosecutors and bailiffs.

    Ref: Texas Penal Code Section 46.03

Unlawful Carrying of a Handgun by a CHL Holder

Senate Bill 60 added section 46.035 to the Penal Code. Act of May 16, 1995, 74th Leg., R.S., ch. 229, §4, 1995 Tex. Sess. Law Serv. 1998, 2013-14. Subsection (b) of section 46.035 provides that a license holder commits an offense if he or she intentionally, knowingly, or recklessly carries a handgun in certain places under the authority of Subchapter H, Chapter 411, Government Code (Concealed Handgun Law). Listed below is unlawful carrying of a handgun by a license holder:

It is an offense if a CHL holder:

1. **Intentionally fails to conceal the handgun.** As a CHL holder you must always conceal your handgun.

    If a concealed handgun licensee is caught carrying a handgun in plain view or if his/her handgun is visible then he/she is subject to criminal charges.

    "Concealed handgun" means: A handgun, the presence of which is not openly discernable to the ordinary observation of a reasonable person.
(An offense under this section is Class A misdemeanor)

Or;

2. **If the CHL holder carries on the premises of a business that has a permit or license issued under Chapter 25, 28, 32, 69, or 74, Alcoholic Beverage Code, if the business derives 51 percent (51%) or more of its income from the sale of service of alcoholic beverages for <u>on-premises consumption</u>, as determined the Texas Alcoholic Beverage Commission under Section 104.06, Alcoholic Beverage Code;**

Never take a handgun into a bar or any other 51% business. If you visit the local bar & grill type establishments i.e. Applebees, Chili's etc, they may or may not be a 51% business. It's the CHL holder's responsibility to look on doors, windows, walls etc for a red colored 51% sign. If you see the sign, immediately return to your vehicle and safely secure your handgun. It is a third degree felony to take the handgun into a 51% business.

3. **On the premises where a high school, collegiate, professional sporting event or interscholastic event is taking place**, unless the license holder is a participant in the event and a handgun is used in the event;
(Class A misdemeanor)

4. **On the premises of a correctional facility**

(Felony in the third degree);

5. **On the premises of a hospital licensed under Chapter 241, Health and Safety Code, or on the premises of a nursing home licensed under Chapter 242, Health and Safety Code**, unless the license holder has written authorization of the hospital or nursing home administration, as appropriate. (Note: does not apply if the actor was not given effective notice under section 30.06) (Class A misdemeanor);

6. **In an amusement park.** "Amusement park" means a permanent indoor or outdoor facility or park where amusement rides are available for use by the public that is located in a county with a population of more than one million, encompasses at least 75 acres in surface area, is enclosed with access only through controlled entries, is open for operation more than 120 days in each calendar year, and has security guards on the premises at all times. The term does not include any public or private driveway, street, sidewalk or walkway, parking lot, parking garage, or other parking area. (Class A misdemeanor)

7. **On the premises of a church, synagogue, or other established place of religious worship.** (Class A misdemeanor) (Note: does not apply if

the actor was not given effective notice under section 30.06);

8. **At any meeting of a governmental entity** (Class A misdemeanor) (Note: does not apply if the actor was not given effective notice under section 30.06);

9. **Or while intoxicated** (Note: According to the Texas Penal Code, it is unlawful for an individual who is intoxicated to carry a handgun.

It is important to note that the Penal Code defines "intoxicated" as not having the normal use of mental or physical faculties by reason of the introduction of alcohol, a controlled substance, a drug, a dangerous drug, a combination of two or more of those substances, or any other substance in the body. **(**See Texas Penal Code 49.01 for more information).

It's a Class A misdemeanor to carry a concealed handgun in the foregoing places, with the exception of the premises of businesses that have permits to sell alcoholic beverages and correctional facilities which are third degree felonies.

The term **"Premises"** as used in section 46.035 "means a building or a portion of a building. The team does not include any public or private driveway, street, sidewalk, walkway, parking lot, parking garage, or other parking area".

The definition of "premises" was added after a witness testified in committee hearings on Senate Bill 60 (March 21, 1995) that case law defines "premises" broadly, to include parking lots, driveways, and land adjacent to a building.

> Ref: Texas Penal Code 46.035

Trespass by a Concealed Handgun License Holder

Ref: Texas Penal Code §30.06

A CHL holder needs to be aware that Section 30.05 of the Texas Penal Code deals with criminal trespass. Under the statue, a person commits the offense of trespass if he enters or remains on or in the property of another without effective consent and he had "notice" that the entry was forbidden or he received "notice" to depart, but failed to do so. Remember that having a Texas CHL does not exempt a person from the basics of the Criminal Trespass Statute (§30.05). A CHL holder can be charged with trespass just like anyone else. Pay close attention to the Texas Penal Code §30.05 in addition to Texas Penal Code§30.06.

Texas Penal Code §30.06 covers trespass by holder of license to carry concealed handgun. A CHL holder commits an offense if the license holder received notice that:

- Entry on the property by a license holder with a concealed handgun was forbidden; or
- Remaining on the property with a concealed handgun was forbidden and failed to depart.

For purposes of this section, a person receives notice if the owner of the property or someone with apparent authority to act for the owner provides notice to the person by **oral or written communication**.

An offense under this section is a Class A misdemeanor.

"Entry" means the intrusion of the entire body. Ref: Entry has the meaning assigned by Section 30.05(b).

"License holder" has the meaning assigned by Section 46.035(f).

In order to provide notice that entry on a property by a license holder with a concealed handgun is forbidden, Penal Code Section 30.06(c) (3) (A) requires that written communication contain the following language:

PROHIBITING HANDGUNS IN A BUSINESS OR OTHER ENTITY

"PURSUANT TO SECTION 30.06, PENAL CODE (TRESPASS BY HOLDER OF A LICENSE TO CARRY A CONCEALED HANDGUN) A PERSON LICENSED UNDER SUBCHAPTER H, CHAPTER 411, GOVERNMENT CODE (CONCEALED HANDGUN LAW), MAY NOT ENTER THIS PROPERTY WITH A CONCEALED HANDGUN."

"CONFORME A LA SECCIÓN 30.06 DEL CÓDIGO PENAL (TRASPASAR PORTANDO ARMAS DE FUEGO) PERSONAS CON LICENCIA BAJO DEL SUB-CAPITULO H, CAPITULO 411, CODIGO DE GOBIERNO (LEY DE PORTAR ARMAS), NO DEBEN ENTRAR A ESTA PROPIEDAD PORTANDO UN ARMA DE FUEGO."

<u>Or</u>

A sign posted on the property that includes the foregoing language in English and Spanish; appears in contrasting colors with block letters at least one inch in height; and is displayed in a conspicuous manner clearly visible to the public.

Penal Code Section 30.06(c) (3) (B) further states that a sign must meet the following requirements:

    i. Includes the language described by Paragraph (A) in both English and Spanish;
    ii. Appears in contrasting colors with block letters at least one inch in height; and
    iii. Is displayed in a conspicuous manner clearly visible to the public.

So as a CHL holder you should look for a 30.06 sign that may be posted before you enter an establishment. If you see a 30.06 sign you may not enter. You should immediately return to your vehicle and safely secure your handgun in a lockable case or by any other means whereas if someone were to break in to your vehicle, they would be unable to steal your handgun.

Most gun stores sell lockable cases that have the ability to be secured by means of a steel cable locking system to ensure someone cannot walk away with the gun case. If you're asked to not enter with a concealed handgun or to leave a property you must abide or you may be charged. Remember "Notice" can be oral or written.

Making a Firearm Accessible To a Child

Ref: Texas Penal Code §46.13

As Americans we enjoy a right that citizens of other countries do not have. We have the right to own firearms but with this right come responsibilities. It is the gun owner's responsibility to ensure that their firearms are stored safely and those unauthorized and untrained individuals cannot gain access to those firearms.

Parents should educate children and family members on what to do if they should find a handgun. As responsible gun owners we should never hide a gun, a child may find it. Be sure to always secure your handgun with a trigger lock, cable lock, or secure it in a lockable gun safe. It may not be your handgun but a neighbor's handgun where your child may play or children may find a handgun on the street where a criminal has ditched a gun. Whatever the case, children are curious! Without the proper education accidents can happen. The National Rifle Association (NRA) has done an outstanding job with their gun safety programs.

One of the NRA's gun safety programs in particular is the Eddie Eagle Gun Safe ® Program. The program teaches children in pre-k through third grade four important steps to take if they find a gun. These steps are presented by the program's mascot, Eddie Eagle ®, in an easy-to-remember format consisting of the following:

If you see a gun: "Stop! Don't Touch, Leave the Area, Tell an Adult."

Texas school districts are authorized under Education Code §21.118 and encouraged to provide firearms safety programs for students in grades K through 12. Children are curious about things they don't understand. In any event, handgun safety education is the key.

Under Texas Penal Code §46.13 a person commit an offense if a child gains access to a readily dischargeable firearm and the person with criminal negligence:

    (1) Failed to secure the firearm; or
    (2) Left the firearm in a place to which the person knew or should have known the child would gain access. In this section a "child" is a person younger than 17 yrs old.

"Secure" means to take steps that a reasonable person would take to prevent the access to a readily dischargeable firearm by a child, including but not limited to placing a firearm in a locked container or temporarily rendering the firearm inoperable by a trigger lock or other means.

"Readily dischargeable firearm" means a firearm that is loaded with ammunition, whether or not a round is in the chamber.

An offense under this section is a Class C misdemeanor. If the child discharges the firearm and causes death or serious bodily injury to himself or another person an offense under this section is a Class A misdemeanor.

It is always the gun owner's responsibility to ensure that unauthorized or untrained individuals cannot gain access to his or her firearms.

Concealed Handgun License Agreements with Other States

Texas establishes CHL agreements with other states. This reciprocity allows Texas CHL holders to carry in the states in which the State of Texas has reciprocity. If you are a Texas CHL holder and you are in another state that has reciprocity with Texas you must follow that state's laws for carrying a concealed handgun. The same responsibility applies to anyone from that other state when traveling in Texas; they must follow the Texas laws for carrying a concealed handgun. Most states will have a website for their concealed carry licenses or permits that will update you on their laws. Alternatively, you may call the other state and ask what their laws are for carrying a concealed handgun while in that state.

It is the CHL holder's responsibility to contact the state in which Texas has reciprocity to find out what the rules are while carrying concealed with a Texas CHL in their respective state. The Texas DPS website is one good place to find out which states recognize the Texas CHL.

Some states on the reciprocity list **Table A-1** recognizes CHLs issued to Texas residents only and do not recognize the licenses issued by Texas to non-residents. In addition, some states only recognize CHL holders that are 21 years of age. I will add a "(*)" to those states with these caveats listed in **Table A-1.**

I have also listed unilateral states in **Table A-2**. The states listed in **Table A-2** do not recognize the Texas CHL however the State of Texas recognizes those states. Therefore they can carry concealed in Texas but Texas CHL holders cannot carry concealed in their respective states.

Under the Statute, Texas may recognize another state's license if their license meets minimal criteria for recognition. The Attorney General will evaluate each state's handgun licensing program to determine whether statutory reciprocity requirements are met. This recognition follows evaluation of the other states licensing statute to see if their law satisfies the minimum criteria. Upon recommendation of the Attorney General, the governor will issue a proclamation or sign a reciprocity agreement recognizing a concealed handgun license issued by another state.

Ref: Texas Government Code 411.173(b) states that " the governor shall negotiate an agreement with any other state that provides for the issuance of a license to carry a concealed handgun under which a license issued by the other state is recognized in this state if the Attorney General of the State of Texas determines that a background check of each applicant for a license issued by that state is initiated by state or local authorities or an agent of the state or local authorities before the license is issued".

For purposes of this subsection, "background check" means a search of the National Crime Information Center database and the Interstate Identification Index maintained by the Federal Bureau of Investigation.

Keep in mind that states may be added or removed without notice and it is the CHL holders' responsibility to visit the Texas DPS website and find out who is on the list.

Texas CHL holders can carry a concealed handgun in those states listed in Table A-1.

Alabama (08-08-2006)	Idaho (08-09-2004)	Montana (11-29-2004)
Alaska (09-26-2005)	Indiana (11-02-2005)	Nebraska (02-16-2007) (*)
Arizona (09-15-1999)	Kansas (01-30-2007) (*)	New Mexico (11-30-2005)
Arkansas (02-19-1998)	Kentucky (08-30-2000)	North Carolina (04-19-2004)
Colorado updated (06-20-2007) (*)	Louisiana (08-31-1998)	North Dakota (02-04-2005)
Delaware (11-01-2005)	Michigan (09-01-2005)(*)	Oklahoma (07-24-1998)
Florida (08-28-2000)	Mississippi (09-07-2004)	Pennsylvania (02-28-2005)
Georgia (11-22-2004)	Missouri (09-06-2005) (*)	South Carolina (02-25-2005)
Tennessee (08-30-2000)	Utah (09-03-2004)	Virginia (09-01-05)
Wyoming (07-25-2002)	South Dakota (06-06-2005)	

[Table A-1 Reciprocal States]

(*Notes):

***Colorado**-Effective May 17, 2007, Colorado will only recognizes permits issued to residents of the issuing state who are at least 21 years of age. Colorado no longer recognizes permits issued to non-residents.

***Kansas**- Effective Jan 30, 2007, Non-Resident Texas Concealed Handgun Licensee's will not be allowed to carry in Kansas.

***Michigan**- Effective Sep 1, 2005, In accordance with Mich. Comp. Laws § 28.432a (f), the State of Michigan may honor valid out-of-state permits held only by residents of a reciprocal state. Therefore, Texas Concealed handgun licenses issued to non-resident Texans under V.T.C.A. GC §411.173 are not eligible for reciprocal recognition.

***Missouri**- The Missouri "permit" is actually a regular Missouri Driver's License or Non-Driver's License issued with a "Concealed Carry Endorsement" on the face of the license. The Endorsement appears in red letters above the license photo and reads "CCW" until (Expiration Date of Endorsement)."

***Nebraska**- Effective Oct 27, 2009, the Texas CHL is recognized in the state of Nebraska. This recognition extends **only** to **Non-Residents** of Nebraska and to individuals **21 years of age and older**. This follows an amendment, effective Aug 30, 2009, to Nebraska law allowing for recognition of out of state licenses. All Texas license holders will be required to follow Nebraska law while carrying in the state. All Nebraska license holders will be required to follow Texas law while carrying in Texas. Texas has recognized Nebraska licenses since Feb 16, 2007.

Texas CHL holders <u>cannot carry in those states listed in table A-2</u> however those states listed in Table A-2 can carry in the State of Texas.

California (11-18-2005)	Connecticut (05-04-2005)
Hawaii (01-13-2006)	Iowa (04-14-2005) <u>**Pending**</u> Senate File 2379-Jan 2011
Maryland (11-18-2005)	Massachusetts (11-18-2005)
Nevada (03-24-2005)	New Jersey (11-18-2005)
New York (01-13-2006)	Rhode Island (01-13-2006)
Washington (11-18-2005)	

[Table A-2 Unilateral Proclamation]

These proclamations are unilateral and are not a reciprocal agreement. Texas CHL holders will not be allowed to carry in those states.

Suspensions and Revocations of the Concealed Handgun License

The Statute clarified that the Department must suspend or revoke a license when the licensee becomes ineligible.

If your license is suspended, it is taken away for a specified period of time or while there is cause for suspension, and returned at the end of a specified period of time or once the cause for suspension no longer exist. Even if the license is not surrendered, the license is deactivated during the period of suspension.

A licensee may be charged with unlawful carrying of a weapon if he/she carries while the license is suspended.

A license is subject to suspension for the following reasons:

- The license holder is charged with the commission of a felony a Class A or B misdemeanor or disorderly conduct.
    - Suspended until the disposition of the charge
- The license holder fails to notify DPS of a change of address or name.
    - Suspended for 30 days

If a license is suspended for a second time for the same reason, the license will be suspended for one to three years.

A court may suspend a license when issuing a protective order. This type of suspension will last for the duration of the protective order.

>Ref: GC §411.187

Revocation of a CHL

If a license is revoked, it is permanently deactivated, even if the license holder does not return the license. If a revoked licensee later becomes eligible, then he/she must reapply as a new applicant.

A CHL is subject to revocation for the following reasons:

- The license holder was not eligible for the license at the time it was issued.
- The license holder gave false information on the application, or failed to disclose a material fact.
- The license holder subsequently becomes ineligible for the license
    - Other than pending charges
- The license holder was convicted of an offense under the Penal Code Section 46.035 "Unlawful Carrying of a Weapon by a license Holder".
- The license holder engages in suspendable conduct after being previously suspended **twice** for the same reason.
- The license holder submits an application fee that is dishonored or reversed if the applicant fails to timely cure the deficiency as outlined the statute.

- o If an applicant's check is returned, the applicant can submit a cashier's check or money order, along with a $25 fee, within 30 days of receiving notification to avoid revocation.
- If a license holder is revoked, he may reapply as a new applicant two years from the anniversary of the date on which the cause for revocation no longer exists.

                Ref: GC §411.186

Texas GC§411.180. Notification of Denial, Revocation, or Suspension of License; Review

(a) The department shall give written notice to each applicant for a CHL of any denial, revocation, suspension of that license.

No later than the 30th day after the notice is received by the applicant, according to the records of the department, the applicant or CHL holder may request a hearing on the denial, revocation, or suspension. The applicant must make a written request for a hearing addressed to the department at its Austin address.

The request for hearing must reach the department in Austin prior to the 30th day after the date of receipt of the written notice.

On receipt of a request for hearing from the CHL holder or applicant, the department shall promptly schedule a hearing in the appropriate justice court in the county of residence of the applicant or CHL holder. The justice court shall conduct a hearing to review the denial, revocation, or suspension of the license. In a proceeding under this section, a justice of the peace shall act as an administrative hearing officer. A hearing under this section is not subject to Chapter 2001 (Administrative

Procedure Act). A district attorney or county attorney, the attorney general, or a designated member of the department may represent the department.

(b) The department, on receipt of a request for hearing, shall file the appropriate petition in the justice court selected for the hearing and send a copy of that petition to the applicant or license holder at the address contained in departmental records. A hearing under this section must be scheduled within 30 days of receipt of the request for a hearing. The hearing shall be held expeditiously but in no event more than 60 days after the date that the applicant or license holder requested the hearing.

The date of the hearing may be reset on the motion of either party, by agreement of the parties, or by the court as necessary to accommodate the court's docket.

(c) The justice court shall determine if the denial, revocation, or suspension is supported by a preponderance of the evidence. Both the applicant or license holder and the department may present evidence. The court shall affirm the denial, revocation, or suspension if the court determines that denial, revocation, or suspension is supported by a preponderance of the evidence. If the court determines that the denial, revocation, or suspension is not supported by a preponderance of the evidence, the court shall order the department to immediately issue or return the license to the applicant or license holder.

(d) A proceeding under this section is subject to Chapter 105, Civil Practice and Remedies Code, relating to fees, expenses, and attorney's fees.

(e) A party adversely affected by the court's ruling following a hearing under this section may appeal the ruling by filing within 30 days after the ruling a petition in a county court at law in the county in which the applicant or license holder resides or, if there is no county court at law in the county, in the county court of the county. A person who appeals under this section must send by certified mail a copy of the person's petition, certified by the clerk of the court in which the petition is filed, to the appropriate division of the department at its Austin headquarters. The trial on appeal shall be a trial de nova without a jury. A district or county attorney or the attorney general may represent the department.

(f) A suspension of a license may not be probated.

(g) If an applicant or a license holder does not petition the justice court, a denial becomes final and a revocation or suspension takes effect on the 30th day after receipt of written notice.

(h) The department may use and introduce into evidence certified copies of governmental records to establish the existence of certain events that could result in the denial, revocation, or suspension of a license under this subchapter, including records regarding convictions, judicial findings regarding mental competency, judicial findings regarding chemical dependency, or other matters that may be established by governmental records that have been properly authenticated.

(i) This section does not apply to a suspension of a license under Section 85.022, Family Code, or Article 17.292, Code of Criminal Procedure.

Use of Force

In the United States the belief in protecting oneself and ones property dates back to colonial times. A quote stated by Richard Henry Lee *"to preserve liberty, it is essential that the whole body of the people always possess arms, and be taught alike, especially when young, how to use them."* Mr. Lee was a Virginia delegate to the Continental Congress, initiator of the declaration of Independence, and a member of the first Senate, which passed the Bill of Rights.

Patrick Henry, in the Virginia Convention on the ratification of the Constitution stated *"The great objective is that every man be armed…Everyone who is able may have a gun."*

James Madison the author of the bill of Rights, in his Federalists Paper No. 46 stated *"The advantage of being armed… The Americans possess over the people of all other nations… Notwithstanding the military establishments in several Kingdoms of Europe, which are carried as far as the public resources will bear, the governments are afraid to trust the people with arms."*

The use of force or deadly force is an action that should not be taken lightly. There is no obligation on any regular citizen to use such force. Deadly force should be used as a means of last resort when you have a fear of loss of life. Always remember that the force applied is intended to

STOP the aggressor. In fact by pulling out a handgun may cause more harm than it is intended to solve.

There are several different force options available for one to consider such as:

- Mental Awareness
- Leave
- Verbal- use of non-violent communication skills
- Non Lethal Options- pepper spray etc.
- Deadly Force Options

Using force should always be the last resort to any situation. Using non-violent dispute resolution is always the best option. The best way to prevent placing oneself in a use/do use situation is to:

- Maintain situational awareness,
- Train as you fight
- Maintain physical and mental preparedness

The use of force by an actor is based on the perceptions that caused him or her to believe the use of force is necessary. The perceptions are formed by:

The Subject Actions + the Circumstances = the Appropriate Force Decision

Some of the factors in determining the use of force include:

- Perception
- Time
- Location
- Your mental/physical preparedness
- Subject Actions
- Subject age, gender, race, ethnicity and size

Have a plan in place and always be aware of your surroundings. It's better to have a plan and not need it than, to need it and not have a plan. Deadly Force is such an important topic and there are consequences for using deadly force.

Now, let's take a look at Chapter 9 of the Texas Penal Code which covers use of force and deadly force.

SELECTED DEADLY FORCE STATUES

This section includes Texas Penal Code Chapter 9 justification excluding criminal responsibility.

PENAL CODE
PC CH.9. JUSTIFICATION EXCLUDING CRIMINAL RESPONSIBILITY

Subchapter A. GENERAL PROVISION

PC §901. DEFINITIONS. In this chapter:
(1) *Custody* has the meaning assigned by Section 38.01.
(2) *Escape* has the meaning assigned by Section 38.01.
(3) *Deadly force* means force that is intended or known by the actor to cause, or in the manner of its use or intended use is capable of causing, death or serious bodily injury.
(4) *Habitation* has the meaning assigned by Section 30.01
(5) *Vehicle* has the meaning assigned by Section 30.01.

PC§9.02. JUSTIFICATION AS A DEFENSE.

It is a defense to prosecution that the conduct in question is justified under this chapter.

PC§9.03. CONFINEMENT AS JUSTIFIABLE FORCE.

Confinement is justified when force is justified by this chapter if the actor takes reasonable measures to terminate the confinement as soon as he knows he safely can unless the person confined has been arrested for an offense.

PC§9.04. THREATS AS JUSTIFIABLE FORCE.

The threat of force is justified when the use of force is justified by this chapter. For purposes of this section, a threat to cause death or serious bodily injury by the production of a weapon or otherwise, as long as the actor's purpose is limited to creating an apprehension that he will use deadly force is necessary, does not constitute the use of deadly force.

PC§9.05. RECKLESS INJURY OF INNOCENT THIRD PERSON.

Even though an actor is justified under this chapter in threatening or using force or deadly force against another, if in doing so he also recklessly injures or kills an innocent third person, the justification afforded by this chapter is unavailable in a prosecution for the reckless injury or killing of the innocent third person.

PC§9.06. CIVIL REMEDIES UNAFFECTED.

The fact that conduct is justified under this chapter does not abolish or impair any remedy for the conduct that is available in a civil suit.

Subchapter B.

JUSTIFICATION GENERALLY

PC §9.21. PUBLIC DUTY.

(a) Except as qualified by Subsections (b) and (c), conduct is justified if the actor reasonably believes the conduct is required or authorized by law, by the judgment or order of a competent court or other governmental tribunal, or in the execution of legal process.

(b) The other sections of this chapter control when force is used against a person to protect persons (Subchapter C), to protect property (Subchapter D), for law enforcement (Subchapter E), or by virtue of a special relationship (Subchapter F).

(c) The use of deadly force is not justified under this section unless the actor reasonably believes the deadly force is specifically required by statute or unless it occurs in the lawful conduct of war. If deadly force is so justified, there is no duty to retreat before using it.

(d) The justification afforded by this section is available if the actor reasonably believes:

(1) The court or governmental tribunal has jurisdiction or the process is lawful, even though the court or

governmental tribunal lacks jurisdiction or the process is unlawful; or

(2) His conduct is required or authorized to assist a public servant in the performance of his official duty, even though the servant exceeds his lawful authority.

PC §9.22. NECESSITY.

Conduct is justified if:

(1) the actor reasonably believes the conduct is immediately necessary to avoid imminent harm;

(2) the desirability and urgency of avoiding the harm clearly outweigh, according to ordinary standards of reasonableness, the harm sought to be prevented by the law proscribing the conduct; and

(3) a legislative purpose to exclude the justification claimed for the conduct does not otherwise plainly appear.

Subchapter. C.

PROTECTION OF PERSONS

PC §9.31. SELF-DEFENSE.

(a) Except as provided in Subsection (b), a person is justified in using force against another when and to the degree the actor reasonably believes the force is immediately necessary to protect the actor against the other's use or attempted use of unlawful force.

The actor's belief that the force was immediately necessary as described by this subsection is presumed to be reasonable if the actor:

(1) knew or had reason to believe that the person against whom the force was used:

>(A) unlawfully and with force entered, or was attempting to enter unlawfully and with force, the actor's occupied habitation, vehicle, or place of business or employment;

>(B) Unlawfully and with force removed, or was attempting to remove unlawfully and with force, the actor from the actor's habitation, vehicle, or place of business or employment; or

>(C) was committing or attempting to commit aggravated kidnapping, murder, sexual assault, aggravated sexual assault, robbery, or aggravated robbery;

(2) did not provoke the person against whom the force was used and

(3) was not otherwise engaged in criminal activity, other than a Class C misdemeanor that is a violation of a law or ordinance regulating traffic at the time the force was used.

(b) **The use of force against another is not justified:**

(1) in response to verbal provocation alone;

(2) to resist an arrest or search that the actor knows is being made by a peace officer, or by a person acting in a peace officer's presence and at his direction, even though the arrest or search is unlawful, unless the resistance is justified under Subsection (c);

(3) if the actor consented to the exact force used or attempted by the other;

(4) if the actor provoked the other's use or attempted use of unlawful force, unless:

> (A) the actor abandons the encounter, or clearly communicates to the other his intent to do so reasonably believing he cannot safely abandon the encounter; and
>
> (B) the other nevertheless continues or attempts to use unlawful force against the actor; or

(5) if the actor sought an explanation from or discussions with the other person concerning the actor's differences with the other person while the actor was:

> (A) carrying a weapon in violation of Section 46.02; or
>
> (B) possessing or transporting a weapon in violation of Section 46.05.

<u>(c) The use of force to resist an arrest or search is justified:</u>

(1) if, before the actor offers any resistance, the peace officer (or person acting at his direction) uses or attempts to use greater force than necessary to make the arrest or search; and

(2) when and to the degree the actor reasonably believes the force is immediately necessary to protect himself against the peace officer's (or other person's) use or attempted use of greater force than necessary.

(d) **The use of deadly force is not justified under this subchapter except as provided in Sections 9.32, 9.33, and 9.34.**

(e) A person who has a right to be present at the location where the force is used, who has not provoked the person against whom the force is used, and who is not engaged in criminal activity at the time the force is used is not required to retreat before using force as described by this section.

(f) For purposes of Subsection (a), in determining whether an actor described by Subsection (e) reasonably believed that the use of force was necessary, a finder of fact may not consider whether the actor failed to retreat.

PC §9.32. DEADLY FORCE IN DEFENSE OF PERSON.

(a) A person is justified in using deadly force against another:

(1) if the actor would be justified in using force against the other under Section 9.31; and

(2) when and to the degree the actor reasonably believes the deadly force is immediately necessary:

> (A) to protect the actor against the other's use or attempted use of unlawful deadly force; or
>
> (B) to prevent the other's imminent commission of aggravated kidnapping, murder, sexual assault, aggravated sexual assault, robbery, or aggravated robbery.

(b) The actor's belief under Subsection (a) (2) that the deadly force was immediately necessary as described by that subdivision is presumed to be reasonable if the actor:

(1) knew or had reason to believe that the person against whom the deadly force was used:

> (A) unlawfully and with force entered, or was attempting to enter unlawfully and with force, the actor's occupied habitation, vehicle, or place of business or employment;

      (B) unlawfully and with force removed, or was attempting to remove unlawfully and with force, the actor from the actor's habitation, vehicle, or place of business or employment; or

      (C) was committing or attempting to commit an offense described by Subsection (a)(2)(B);

(2) did not provoke the person against whom the force was used; and

(3) was not otherwise engaged in criminal activity, other than a Class C misdemeanor that is a violation of a law or ordinance regulating traffic at the time the force was used.

(c) A person who has a right to be present at the location where the deadly force is used, who has not provoked the person against whom the deadly force is used, and who is not engaged in criminal activity at the time the deadly force is used is not required to retreat before using deadly force as described by this section.

(d) For purposes of Subsection (a) (2), in determining whether an actor described by Subsection (c) reasonably believed that the use of deadly force was necessary, a finder of fact may not consider whether the actor failed to retreat.

PC §9.33. DEFENSE OF THIRD PERSON.

A person is justified in using force or deadly force against another to protect a third person if:

(1) under the circumstances as the actor reasonably believes them to be, the actor would be justified under Section 9.31 or 9.32 in using force or deadly force to protect himself against the unlawful force or unlawful deadly force he reasonably believes to be threatening the third person he seeks to protect; and

(2) the actor reasonably believes that his intervention is immediately necessary to protect the third person.

PC §9.34. PROTECTION OF LIFE OR HEALTH.

(a) A person is justified in using force, but not deadly force, against another when and to the degree he reasonably believes the force is immediately necessary to prevent the other from committing suicide or inflicting serious bodily injury to himself.

(b) A person is justified in using both force and deadly force against another when and to the degree he reasonably believes the force or deadly force is immediately necessary to preserve the other's life in an emergency.

PC §9.41.
PROTECTION OF ONE'S OWN PROPERTY.

(a) A person in lawful possession of land or tangible, movable property is justified in using force against another when and to the degree the actor reasonably believes the force is immediately necessary to prevent or terminate the other's trespass on the land or unlawful interference with the property.

(b) A person unlawfully dispossessed of land or tangible, movable property by another is justified in using force against the other when and to the degree the actor reasonably believes the force is immediately necessary to reenter the land or recover the property if the actor uses the force immediately or in fresh pursuit after the dispossession and:

    (1) the actor reasonably believes the other had no claim of right when he dispossessed the actor; or

    (2) the other accomplished the dispossession by using force, threat, or fraud against the actor.

PC §9.42.
DEADLY FORCE TO PROTECT PROPERTY.

A person is justified in using deadly force against another to protect land or tangible, movable property:

(1) if he would be justified in using force against the other under
Section 9.41; and

(2) when and to the degree he reasonably believes the deadly force is immediately necessary:

    (A) to prevent the other's imminent commission of arson, burglary, robbery, aggravated robbery, theft during the nighttime, or criminal mischief during the nighttime; or

    (B) to prevent the other who is fleeing immediately after committing burglary, robbery, aggravated robbery, or theft during the nighttime from escaping with the property; and

(3) he reasonably believes that:

    (A) the land or property cannot be protected or recovered by any other means; or

    (B) the use of force other than deadly force to protect or recover the land or property would expose the actor or another to a substantial risk of death or serious bodily injury.

PC §9.43. PROTECTION OF THIRD PERSON'S PROPERTY.

A person is justified in using force or deadly force against another to protect land or tangible, movable property of a third person if, under the circumstances as he reasonably believes them to be, the actor would be justified under Section 9.41 or 9.42 in using force or deadly force to protect his own land or property and:

(1) the actor reasonably believes the unlawful interference constitutes attempted or consummated theft of or criminal mischief to the tangible movable property; or

(2) the actor reasonably believes that:

> A. the third person has requested his protection of the land or property;
>
> B. he has a legal duty to protect the third person's land or property; or
>
> C. the third person whose land or property he uses force or deadly force to protect is the actor's spouse, parent, or child, resides with the actor, or is under the actor's care.

PC §9.44. USE OF DEVICE TO PROTECT PROPERTY.

The justification afforded by Sections 9.41 and 9.43 applies to the use of a device to protect land or tangible, movable property if:

(1) the device is not designed to cause, or known by the actor to create a substantial risk of causing, death or serious bodily injury; and

(2) use of the device is reasonable under all the circumstances as the actor reasonably believes them to be when he installs the device.

Non-Violent Dispute Resolution

Non-violent dispute resolution is very important as is relates to carrying a firearm and the ability to handle conflict situations in a peaceful manner. It's all part of the communication process.

As a society, we have developed ways to exchange information in order to express what we want, what we need, how we feel etc… But in order for communication to be effective, we must know how to get our message across. In conflict situations, people tend to focus on the anger and the blame. Time is wasted on accusations and harsh words. When this occurs, the initial purpose of the conversation is lost. Resentment, frustration and sometimes violence can erupt causing emotional and physical injuries. In more severe instances, even death can result. This can be due to the failure to communicate.

Communication can fail when we do not look at each other when speaking or when we do not listen to what is being said and when we do not respond with the appropriate words to make sure that the message was received correctly. Communication or lack of between people can cause problems. There are four common elements of a conversation:

- The Speaker
- The Message
- The Receiver
- Feed back.

"Feedback" is the most important element in a conversation. It is the most important, because it lets us know that the message was received correctly. Especially in states such as Texas where English and Spanish are prominent languages.

In the communication process we have Verbal, Non-verbal and barriers to effective communication.

Verbal Communication

When people talk to each other, there are actually six different interactions taking place between the speaker and the listener.

There are two interactions when a message is sent:

1. What the speaker intends to say
2. What the speaker actually said

Three more interactions occur with:

3. What the receiver heard

4. What the receiver thinks was heard

5. What the receiver responds back to the speaker

The last interaction is:

6. What the speaker thinks was said by the receiver

And the cycle begins again. So a person can see that there are six opportunities for information to become lost or misunderstood.

Non-Verbal Communication

While people are talking to each other, not only are words exchanged but there are silent signs, signals and behaviors that are communicated. Information can be received negatively through:

- Facial Expressions

- Body Position

- Eye Contact (or lack of)

- Appearance

- Touch

- Voice Tone, and

- Hand Gestures

Sometimes these silent communicators cause the original information to be received incorrectly. These non-verbal signals or signs can be deceiving. Good intentions and good verbal skills can be lost among the negative non-verbal.

Barriers

There are several barriers to effective communication. A number of things can interfere with what a person is trying to say and with how a person hears what is being said. Barriers can be created intentionally or unintentionally. The trick is to identify those barriers and work around them to prevent unnecessary anger and frustration in the communication efforts. Listed are some common barriers:

1. Background of People
2. Assumptions
3. Poor Listening
4. Previous Interactions
5. Other Indications

Background of People: Customs, accents, language usage or the inability to understand the English language can prevent a person from comprehending what someone is actually trying to say.

Assumptions: The work environment, home environment and even stable relationships can all create a foundation of assumptions. If an assumption is made before the initial information is completed, the potential for misinformation is likely.

Poor Listening: There are those people who are just not good listeners. They will not devote the time necessary to get the correct information. Such people create their own barriers to communication by not putting their issues aside and focusing on what is being said by others.

Previous Interactions: If people have had problems with each other in the past, there is potential for conflict because of these past issues. If communication is to be valued and respected, previous disagreements or arguments must not become part of the interaction.

Other Indications: Watching your listeners can give you an insight into how they are receiving your information. Facial expressions showing signs of confusion, disinterest or lack of attention may provide insight. Be aware of what is going on and make adjustments to these barriers.

In 1964 Dr. Eric Berne wrote in his book "Games People Play" that we are all composed of three (3) separate "selves". According to Dr. Berne we are composed of a Parent-Adult-Child ego state and at any given moment an individual in a social situation will exhibit one of these ego states, and individuals can shift with varying degrees of readiness from one ego state to another.

In the parent ego state, you are in the same state of mind as one of your parents used to be, and you are responding as he/she would with the same posture, gestures, vocabulary, feelings etc. In conflict situation, we say things like "Hey you shouldn't do that" or "You should know better". A person should pay attention and never be in this state of mind as it causes conflict. No one wants to be talked to in this manner.

In the child ego state your reaction in a conflict situation is the same as it would have been when you were a little boy or girl. We say things like "I'll do it if I feel like it" "I don't have to" or "You can't make me." We should never be in this state of mind as it to causes conflict.

In a situation that induces conflict, our parent and child selves become pretty dominate. We become self-consumed and all we are concerned with is "I, me and my". These personal, possessive pronouns are a real danger sign and work to cut out all of our adult perspectives.

In the Adult ego state, you have made an objective appraisal of the situation and are using the thoughts processes, or the problems you perceive, or the conclusions you have come to, in a non-prejudicial manner. As adults we use pronouns such as "we""us" and "our". We share the blame for example: *Maybe we just got a little out of hand, let's just forget about it.*

According to Dr. Berne, the single best way to stop conflict and the only way to resolve conflict is to speak to a person in an adult-to-adult mode.

This works to diffuse conflict by not allowing a person to get on the defensive and by letting them keep their dignity, self-respect and save face. A person carrying a firearm for self defense should always be in the adult ego state of mind.

Bad communication habits follow us through our lives and eventually make us believe that it is the fault of everyone else when communication goes wrong. There are three (3) common mistakes that provide a breeding ground for anger, resentment, and frustration. These mistakes cause communication to become less effective.

1. Moralistic Judgments- We make judgments of others to make us feel better about why everything went wrong. We imply that people that don't agree with us are wrong. Language used in these judgments includes "selfish", "lazy" "idiots", etc. Blame, insults, criticism and comparisons are forms of judgment. Think in terms of others behaving in certain ways, we react in terms of their wrongness.

2. Making Comparisons- We compare others to what we would do in similar situations. By doing so we justify our anger by claiming that others did not do it the way we would have done it.

3. Denial of Responsibility- Blaming everyone and everything else. Accepting no responsibility for the problem and claiming that the response or action was "because I had to…" People make this mistake because they use language that implies a lack of choice rather than using language that acknowledges choice.

Dr. Marshall Rosenberg lists four (4) components to using the non-violent way of communicating in his book *"Non-Violent Communication: A Language of Life"* that I believe everyone should learn and by remembering these components, we can identify the potential for conflict and remain in a neutral position. Follow these components and we can be successful in preventing a conflict situation from getting out of hand and remain in control of ourselves.

1. Observe without evaluating

2. Express your feelings

3. Acknowledge what you need

4. Make your request

Observe without evaluating- As an adult in a conflict situation we should observe what the conflict is without placing blame or participate in name-calling. Time is wasted on determining whose fault it is and why it happened. Focus on the problem or conflict and getting it resolved.

Express what you are feeling-Are you concerned about certain issues? Are you frustrated, angry and sad? Dr. Rosenberg has two lists in his book that provides words to use when one's needs are or are not being met.

Acknowledge what you need-We have not learned how to think about what we need when involved in a conflict. We have a tendency to, once again, resort to placing blame for our anger on the others involved. Many times it is our expectations of people to know what it is we need that escalated our anger. By taking the initiative and verbally expressing what we feel and what we need, most of our personal anger can be eliminated.

Make your request-We tend to expect others to know what we want without us verbally expressing it. This creates conflict situations. By making known what we want in return can remove the guess work and move the communication in a positive direction.

Keys to help redirect negative behavior

Acronym

A. **Listen**- One of the most important communication skills known to man.

1. **L**-Look at the person

2. **I**- Show an interest

3. **S**-Summarize what was said and repeat it back

4. **T**-(Territory) Keep a comfortable space

5. **E**-Empathize, try to see if from their perspective

6. **N**-Nod to show that you are trying to understand

B. **Empathize**-The dictionary defines this as to understand/share in another's emotions or feelings.

C. **Ask**-Asking questions helps a person to redirect from reaction to response, it builds rapport and eases tension.

D. **Paraphrase**-a backup system to effective communication, put the person's meaning into your own words and give it back to them, correct any misconceptions.

E. **Summarize**-Putting it all together. After listening to what was said, asking questions, clarifying what was heard by repeating the message back in your own words, and correcting any misconceptions, you will finally say, "As I am understanding you, you are saying that…"

Common signs of emotional disturbance include:

1. Clinched or clinching fists

2. Increased deep and rapid respiration

3. Sweating

4. Elevated blood pressure (red face/complexion)

5. Violent verbal outburst

6. Crying

7. Tantrum like behavior

8. Body tremors (shaking)

9. Stuttering speech, and

10. Intense or fixed eye contact on a target or focal point (such as perceived source of stress).

All signs come from two sources:

- Physiological-Body
- Psychological-Mind

Somehow, some way we physically exhibit our stress, tension and anger.

Conflict De-Escalation Techniques

There are four elements in a confrontation that must be analyzed and understood by any citizen who carries a firearm is **P.A.C.E**

Acronym

1. **P**- Problem- What has brought about the conflict?

2. **A**-Audience- Who are the actual players involved? Where are they from? Are there any cultural differences and similarities?

3. **C**-Constraints- Are there any barriers to effective communication?

4. **E**-Ethical Presence-This is a total expression of self control. Using the four components of non-violent communication can assist with this effort.

In summary, we discussed Interactions of a Conversation; Verbal, Non-Verbal and Barriers; the (3) Ego States: Parent-Adult-Child; Keys to Redirecting Negative Behavior: The L.I.S.T.E.N.S. acronym; Common Signs of Emotional Disturbance: Physiological and Psychological; and Conflict De-Escalation Techniques: P.A.C.E.

Be aware of what you say, how you say it, and focus on solving the problem.

Carry Safely!

References:

- <u>Non-Violent Communication: A Language of Life</u>, Marshall B. Rosenberg, Ph.D. Puddle Dancer Press, Encinitas, CA 2003

- <u>How to Solve Communication Problems</u>, Fred Pryor Seminar, April 1992

- <u>Effective Communication</u>, Sergeant Starlane Riddle, Texas Department of Public Safety, Training Academy

- <u>Verbal Judo-The Gentle Art of Persuasion,</u> George J. Thompson, Ph.D. and Jerry B. Jenkins, (William Morrow and Company, Inc. New York, NY, 1993)

- Instructor Presentations, *Texas Department of Public Safety*. Retrieved January 10, 2012, from http://www.txdps.state.tx.us/administration/crime_records/chl/instrguidepres.htm

Texas Department of Public Safety contact information

The Texas DPS Concealed Handgun Contact Center is open Monday through Friday 8:00 AM – 5:00 PM and can be reached by phone at: (512) 424-7293.

Mail your completed CHL documents **if you are not including payment** to the Texas DPS address of:

> Concealed Handgun Licensing MSC 0245
> Regulatory Services Division
> Texas Department of Public Safety
> PO Box 4087
> Austin, Texas 78773-0245

If you **are including payment** send to the following:

> Texas Department of Public Saf
> PO Box 15888
> Austin, TX 78761-5888

A person may also contact Texas DPS by email. Just visit the Texas DPS website and click the "Contact Us" link.

www.txdps.state.tx.us

Click on services/regulatory services and then concealed handgun to visit the DPS CHL home page.

Laws Relating To the TEXAS CHL Quick Reference List

GOVERNMENT CODE
CH. 411. TEXAS DEPARTMENT OF PUBLIC SAFETY
Subchapter. H. LICENSE TO CARRY A CONCEALED HANDGUN

§411.171. DEFINITIONS
§411.1711. CERTAIN EXEMPTIONS FROM CONVICTIONS
§411.172. ELIGIBILITY
§411.173. NONRESIDENT LICENSE
§411.174. APPLICATION
§411.175. REQUEST FOR APPLICATION MATERIALS
§411.176. REVIEW OF APPLICATION MATERIALS
§411.177. ISSUANCE OR DENIAL OF LICENSE
§411.178. NOTICE TO LOCAL LAW ENFORCEMENT
§411.179. FORM OF LICENSE
§411.180. NOTIFICATION OF DENIAL, REVOCATION, OR SUSPENSION OF LICENSE; REVIEW

§411.181. NOTICE OF CHANGE OF ADDRESS OR NAME
§411.182. NOTICE
§411.183. EXPIRATION
§411.184. MODIFICATION
§411.185. RENEWAL
§411.186. REVOCATION
§411.187. SUSPENSION OF LICENSE
§411.188. HANDGUN PROFICIENCY REQUIREMENT
§411.1881. EXEMPTION FROM INSTRUCTION FOR CERTAIN PERSONS
§411.1882. EVIDENCE OF HANDGUN PROFICIENCY FOR CERTAIN PERSONS
§411.189. HANDGUN PROFICIENCY CERTIFICATE
§411.190. QUALIFIED HANDGUN INSTRUCTORS
§411.191. REVIEW OF DENIAL, REVOCATION, OR SUSPENSION OF CERTIFICATION AS QUALIFIED HANDGUN INSTRUCTOR

§411.192. CONFIDENTIALITY OF RECORDS

§411.193. STATISTICAL REPORT
§411.194. REDUCTION OF FEES DUE TO INDIGENCY
§411.195. REDUCTION OF FEES FOR SENIOR CITIZENS
§411.1951. WAIVER OR REDUCTION OF FEES FOR MEMBERS OR VETERANS OF UNITED STATES ARMED FORCES

§411.196. METHOD OF PAYMENT
§411.197. RULES
§411.198. LAW ENFORCEMENT OFFICER ALIAS HANDGUN LICENSE

§411.199. HONORABLY RETIRED PEACE OFFICERS
§411.1991. ACTIVE PEACE OFFICERS
§411.200. APPLICATION TO LICENSED SECURITY OFFICERS

§411.201. ACTIVE AND RETIRED JUDICIAL OFFICERS
§411.202. LICENSE A BENEFIT
§411.203. RIGHTS OF EMPLOYERS
§411.204. NOTICE REQUIRED ON CERTAIN PREMISES
§411.205. REQUIREMENT TO DISPLAY LICENSE
§411.206. SEIZURE OF HANDGUN AND LICENSE
§411.207. AUTHORITY OF PEACE OFFICER TO DISARM
§411.208. LIMITATION OF LIABILITY
==============================
HEALTH & SAFETY CODE
§12.092. MEDICAL ADVISORY BOARD; BOARD MEMBERS
§12.095. BOARD PANELS; POWERS AND DUTIES
§12.097. CONFIDENTIALITY REQUIREMENTS
==============================

PENAL CODE
§30.05. CRIMINAL TRESPASS
§30.06. TRESPASS BY HOLDER OF LICENSE TO CARRY CONCEALED HANDGUN
§38.01. DEFINITIONS
§42.01. DISORDERLY CONDUCT

CHAPTER. 46. WEAPONS
§46.01. DEFINITIONS
§46.02. UNLAWFUL CARRYING WEAPONS
§46.03. PLACES WEAPONS PROHIBITED
§46.035. UNLAWFUL CARRYING OF HANDGUN BY LICENSE HOLDER
§46.04. UNLAWFUL POSSESSION OF FIREARM
§46.041. UNLAWFUL POSSESSION OF METAL OR BODY ARMOR BY FELON
§46.05. PROHIBITED WEAPONS
§46.06. UNLAWFUL TRANSFER OF CERTAIN WEAPONS
§46.07. INTERSTATE PURCHASE
§46.08. HOAX BOMBS
§46.09. COMPONENTS OF EXPLOSIVES
§46.10. DEADLY WEAPON IN PENAL INSTITUTION
§46.11. PENALTY IF OFFENSE COMMITTED WITHIN WEAPON-FREE SCHOOL ZONE
§46.12. MAPS AS EVIDENCE OF LOCATION OR AREA
§46.13. MAKING A FIREARM ACCESSIBLE TO A CHILD
§46.15. NONAPPLICABILITY

SELECTED DEADLY FORCE STATUTES PENAL CODE CHAPTER. 9. JUSTIFICATION EXCLUDING CRIMINAL RESPONSIBILITY
Subchapter. A GENERAL PROVISIONS
§9.01. DEFINITIONS
§9.02. JUSTIFICATION AS A DEFENSE
§9.03. CONFINEMENT AS JUSTIFIABLE FORCE
§9.04. THREATS AS JUSTIFIABLE FORCE
§9.05. RECKLESS INJURY OF INNOCENT THIRD PERSON
§9.06. CIVIL REMEDIES UNAFFECTED

Subchapter. B. JUSTIFICATION GENERALLY
§9.21. PUBLIC DUTY
§9.22. NECESSITY

Subchapter. C. PROTECTION OF PERSONS
§9.31. SELF-DEFENSE
§9.32. DEADLY FORCE IN DEFENSE OF PERSON
§9.33. DEFENSE OF THIRD PERSON
§9.34. PROTECTION OF LIFE OR HEALTH

Subchapter. D. PROTECTION OF PROPERTY
§9.41. PROTECTION OF ONE'S OWN PROPERTY
§9.42. DEADLY FORCE TO PROTECT PROPERTY
§9.43. PROTECTION OF THIRD PERSON'S PROPERTY
§9.44. USE OF DEVICE TO PROTECT PROPERTY

Subchapter. E. LAW ENFORCEMENT
§9.51. ARREST AND SEARCH
§9.52. PREVENTION OF ESCAPE FROM CUSTODY
§9.53. MAINTAINING SECURITY IN CORRECTIONAL FACILITY

Subchapter. F. SPECIAL RELATIONSHIPS
§9.61. PARENT--CHILD
§9.62. EDUCATOR--STUDENT
§9.63. GUARDIAN--INCOMPETENT
============================

CODE OF CRIMINAL PROCEDURE
Art. 17.292(l). MAGISTRATES ORDER FOR EMERGENCY PROTECTION
=============
EDUCATION CODE
§37.125. EXHIBITION OF FIREARMS
==============
FAMILY CODE
§58.003. SEALING OF RECORDS
§85.022. REQUIREMENTS OF ORDER APPLYING TO PERSON WHO COMMITTED FAMILY VIOLENCE
==============

GOVERNMENT CODE
§76.0051. AUTHORIZATION TO CARRY WEAPON
§411.047. REPORTING RELATED TO CONCEALED HANDGUN INCIDENTS
=====================
HUMAN RESOURCE CODE
§80.001. FINGERPRINTING FOR IDENTIFICATION
=====================
LOCAL GOVERNMENT CODE
§229.001. FIREARMS; EXPLOSIVES
§250.001. RESTRICTION ON REGULATION OF SPORT SHOOTING RANGES
=====================
LABOR CODE
Subchapter. G. RESTRICTIONS ON PROHIBITING EMPLOYEE TRANSPORTATION OR STORAGE OF CERTAIN FIREARMS
§52.061. RESTRICTIONS ON PROHIBITING EMPLOYEE ACCESS TO OR STORAGE OF FIREARM OR AMMUNITION
§52.062. EXEMPTIONS
§52.063. IMMUNITY FROM CIVIL LIABILITY

=====================

CIVIL PRACTICE AND REMEDIES CODE (CPRC)

CPRC CHAPTER. 83. USE OF DEADLY FORCE IN DEFENSE OF PERSON
§ 83.001. CIVIL IMMUNITY

ABOUT THE AUTHOR

Bernard Lawson is retired from the United States Army and is a disabled veteran who has a love for handguns. He is also a Texas Department of Public Safety Certified Concealed Handgun Instructor and holds certifications in Large & Small Group Instruction from the Department of Defense. In addition he has completed the Texas Commission on Law Enforcement Officer Standards and Education Firearms Instructors Course# 2222.

Send all inquiries to bernard@texaschlacademy.com

Made in the USA
San Bernardino, CA
03 January 2013